Financial Accounting: Preparing Financial Statements

Workbook

David Cox

Published by Osborne Books Limited
Tel 01905 748071
Email books@osbornebooks.co.uk
Website www.osbornebooks.co.uk

Design by Laura Ingham

Printed by CPI Group (UK) Limited, Croydon, CR0 4YY, on environmentally friendly, acid-free paper from managed forests.

British Library Cataloguing in Publication Data
A catalogue record for this book is available from the British Library

ISBN 978-1-911681-01-4

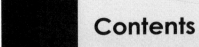

Contents

Introduction

Chapter activities

Practice assessments

Answers to practice assessments

Introduction

what this book covers

This book has been written specifically to cover the Unit 'Financial Accounting: Preparing Financial Statements' which is mandatory for the following qualifications:

AAT Level 3 Diploma in Accounting

AAT Level 3 Certificate in Bookkeeping

AAT Diploma in Accounting – SCQF Level 7

The book contains a clear text with worked examples and case studies, chapter summaries and key terms to help with revision. Each chapter concludes with a wide range of activities, many in the style of AAT computer based assessments.

Osborne Study and Revision Materials

Additional materials, tailored to the needs of students studying this unit and revising for the assessment, include:

- **Tutorials:** paperback books with practice activities
- **Wise Guides:** pocket-sized spiral bound revision cards
- **Student Zone:** access to Osborne Books online resources
- **Osborne Books App:** Osborne Books ebooks for mobiles and tablets

Visit www.osbornebooks.co.uk for details of study and revision resources and access to online material.

Chapter activities

1   The accounting system

1.1   Fill in the missing words to the following sentences:

(a)   The [　　　　　　　] accountant is mainly concerned with external reporting.

(b)   The sales day book is an example of a book of [　　　　　　　] [　　　　　　　].

(c)   Receivables ledger contains the personal accounts of [　　　　　　　] [　　　　　　　].

(d)   Sales account is contained in the [　　　　　　　] ledger.

(e)   Income minus [　　　　　　　] equals [　　　　　　　].

(f)   [　　　　　　　] minus [　　　　　　　] equals capital.

1.2   In an accounting system, which **one** of the following represents the most logical sequence?

(a)	Book of prime entry; financial document; double-entry bookkeeping; trial balance; financial statements (final accounts)
(b)	Financial document; book of prime entry; double-entry bookkeeping; trial balance; financial statements (final accounts)
(c)	Financial document; book of prime entry; double-entry bookkeeping; financial statements (final accounts); trial balance
(d)	Financial document; double-entry bookkeeping; book of prime entry; trial balance; financial statements (final accounts)

1.3 Write out the figures which make up the accounting equation (assets – liabilities = capital) after each of the following consecutive transactions (ignore VAT):

- Owner starts in business with capital of £10,000 comprising £9,000 in the bank and £1,000 in cash.

- Purchases office equipment for £2,500, paid from the bank.

- A friend lends £2,000, paid into the bank.

- Purchases machinery for £8,000, paid from the bank.

- Purchases office equipment for £2,000 on credit from Wyvern Office Supplies.

1.4 Fill in the missing figures:

	Assets £	Liabilities £	Capital £
(a)	10,000	0	....
(b)	20,000	7,500	....
(c)	16,750	....	10,500
(d)	....	4,350	12,680
(e)	17,290	....	11,865
(f)	....	6,709	17,294

1.5   The table below sets out account balances from the books of a business. The columns (a) to (f) show the account balances resulting from a series of transactions that have taken place over time. **You are to** compare each set of adjacent columns – ie (a) with (b), (b) with (c), and so on – and state, with figures, what accounting transactions have taken place in each case. (Ignore VAT.)

	(a)	(b)	(c)	(d)	(e)	(f)
	£	£	£	£	£	£
Assets						
Office equipment	–	5,000	5,000	5,500	5,500	5,500
Machinery	–	–	–	–	6,000	6,000
Bank	7,000	2,000	7,000	7,000	1,000	3,000
Cash	1,000	1,000	1,000	500	500	500
Liabilities						
Loan	–	–	5,000	5,000	5,000	5,000
Capital	8,000	8,000	8,000	8,000	8,000	10,000

2 Double-entry bookkeeping

Note: a set of photocopiable blank ledger accounts is printed in the Appendix of *Financial Accounting: Preparing Financial Statements Tutorial*, and is also available in the Products and Resources section of www.osbornebooks.co.uk.

2.1 Fill in the missing words to the following sentences:

(a) A [   ] entry records an account which gains value, or records an asset, or an expense.

(b) In the books of a business, the [   ] side of bank account records money paid out.

(c) In capital account, the initial capital contributed by the owner of the business is recorded on the [   ] side.

(d) Office equipment is an example of a [   ] asset.

(e) The purchase of a printer for use in the office is classed as [   ] expenditure.

(f) Repairs to a printer are classed as [   ] expenditure.

2.2   The following are the business transactions of Andrew King (who is not registered for VAT) for the month of October 20-4:

1 Oct	Started in business with capital of £7,500 in the bank
4 Oct	Purchased a machine for £4,000, paying by bank transfer
6 Oct	Purchased office equipment for £2,250, paying by bank transfer
11 Oct	Paid rent £400, by bank transfer
12 Oct	Received a loan of £1,500 from a friend, Tina Richards, paid into the bank
15 Oct	Paid wages £500, by bank transfer
18 Oct	Commission received £200, by bank transfer
20 Oct	Drawings £250, by bank transfer
25 Oct	Paid wages £450, by bank transfer

You are to:

(a)   Write up Andrew King's bank account.

(b)   Complete the double-entry bookkeeping transactions.

2.3   The purchase of goods for resale on credit is recorded in the accounts as:

	Debit	Credit	
(a)	Trade payables account	Purchases account	
(b)	Purchases account	Cash account	
(c)	Purchases account	Trade payables account	
(d)	Trade payables account	Sales account	

2.4   Unsatisfactory goods, which were purchased on credit, are returned to the supplier. This is recorded in the accounts as:

	Debit	**Credit**	
(a)	Sales returns account	Trade payables account	
(b)	Purchases returns account	Trade payables account	
(c)	Trade payables account	Purchases returns account	
(d)	Trade payables account	Purchases account	

2.5   For each transaction below, complete the table to show the accounts which will be debited and credited:

(a)   Purchased goods, paying from the bank.

(b)   Payment received for cash sales, paid into the bank.

(c)   Purchased goods on credit from Teme Traders.

(d)   Sold goods on credit to L Harris.

(e)   Returned unsatisfactory goods to Teme Traders.

(f)   L Harris returns unsatisfactory goods.

(g)   Received a loan from D Perkins, paid into the bank.

(h)   Withdrew cash from the bank for use in the business.

Note: ignore Value Added Tax.

Transaction	Account debited	Account credited
(a)		
(b)		
(c)		
(d)		
(e)		
(f)		
(g)		
(h)		

2.6   The following are the business transactions of Pershore Packaging for the month of January 20-8:

4 Jan	Purchased goods, £250, on credit from AB Supplies Limited
5 Jan	Sold goods, £195, a bank transfer received
7 Jan	Sold goods, £150, cash received
11 Jan	Received a loan of £1,000 from J Johnson, paid into the bank
15 Jan	Paid £250 to AB Supplies Limited by bank transfer
18 Jan	Sold goods, £145, on credit to L Lewis
20 Jan	Purchased goods, £225, paying by bank transfer
22 Jan	Paid wages, £125, in cash
26 Jan	Purchased office equipment, £160, on credit from Mercia Office Supplies Limited
28 Jan	Received a bank transfer for £145 from L Lewis
29 Jan	Paid the amount owing to Mercia Office Supplies Limited by bank transfer

You are to record the transactions in the books of account.

Notes:

- Pershore Packaging is not registered for Value Added Tax.

- Day books are not required.

2.7   Enter the following transactions into the double-entry accounts of Sonya Smith:

20-6

2 Feb	Purchased goods £200, on credit from G Lewis
4 Feb	Sold goods £150, on credit to L Jarvis
8 Feb	Sold goods £240, on credit to G Patel
10 Feb	Paid G Lewis the amount owing by bank transfer after deducting a prompt payment discount of 5%
12 Feb	L Jarvis pays the amount owing by bank transfer after deducting a prompt payment discount of 2%
17 Feb	Purchased goods £160, on credit from G Lewis
19 Feb	G Patel pays the amount owing by bank transfer after deducting a prompt payment discount of 2.5%
24 Feb	Paid G Lewis the amount owing by bank transfer after deducting a prompt payment discount of 5%

Notes:

- Sonya Smith is not registered for Value Added Tax.

- Day books are not required.

3 Balancing accounts and the trial balance

Note: a set of photocopiable blank ledger accounts is printed in the Appendix of *Financial Accounting: Preparing Financial Statements Tutorial*, and is also available in the Products and Resources section of www.osbornebooks.co.uk.

3.1   Which **one** of the following accounts normally has a debit balance?

(a)	Loan	
(b)	Bank overdraft	
(c)	Sales	
(d)	Purchases	

3.2   Which **one** of the following accounts normally has a credit balance?

(a)	Drawings	
(b)	Capital	
(c)	Cash	
(d)	Premises	

3.3   Prepare the trial balance of Tina Wong as at 30 November 20-9.

	£
Bank overdraft	1,855
Capital	9,000
Cash	85
Office equipment	2,500
Purchases	2,419
Purchases returns	102
Sales	4,164
Sales returns	354
Trade payables	1,082
Trade receivables	2,115
Vehicle	7,500
Wages	1,230

3.4   The bookkeeper of Lorna Fox has extracted the following list of balances as at 31 March 20-1:

	£
Administration expenses	10,240
Bank overdraft	1,050
Capital	155,440
Cash	150
Drawings	9,450
Interest paid	2,350
Loan from bank	20,000
Machinery	40,000
Premises	125,000
Purchases	96,250
Sales	146,390
Sales returns	8,500
Telephone	3,020
Trade payables	10,545
Trade receivables	10,390
Travel expenses	1,045
Value Added Tax (amount owing to HM Revenue & Customs)	1,950
Wages	28,980

You are to:

(a)   Produce the trial balance at 31 March 20-1.

(b)   Take any three debit balances and any three credit balances and explain to someone who does not understand accounting why they are listed as such, and what this means to the business.

3.5   Fill in the missing words to the following sentences:

(a)   "You made an error of [   ] when you debited the cost of

fuel for the van to Vans Account."

(b)   "There is a 'bad figure' on a purchases invoice – we have read it as £35 when it should be

£55. It has gone through our accounts wrongly so we have an error of [   ]

[   ] to put right."

(c)   "Who was in charge of that trainee last week? He has entered the payment for the electricity

bill on the debit side of the bank and on the credit side of electricity – a [   ]

of [   ]."

(d)   "I found this purchase invoice from last week in amongst the copy statements. As we haven't

put it through the accounts we have an error of [   ]."

(e)   "I've had the bookkeeper from D Jones Limited on the 'phone concerning the statements of

account that we sent out the other day. She says that there is a sales invoice charged that

she knows nothing about. I wonder if we have made an error of [   ]

and it should be for T Jones' account?"

3.6   The following are the business transactions of Mark Tansall, a computer consultant and retailer, for the months of January and February 20-4:

Transactions for January

20-4

1 Jan	Started in business with capital of £10,000 in the bank
4 Jan	Paid rent on premises £500, by bank transfer
5 Jan	Purchased shop fittings £5,000, paid by bank transfer
7 Jan	Purchased goods for resale, £7,500, on credit from Tech Software
11 Jan	Sales £2,400, paid into bank
12 Jan	Sales £2,000, paid into bank
16 Jan	Purchased goods for resale £5,000, on credit from Datasoft Limited
20 Jan	Sales £1,500 to Wyvern School, a bank transfer received
22 Jan	Sales £2,250, paid into bank
25 Jan	Purchased goods for resale from A & A Supplies £3,000, paid by bank transfer
27 Jan	Wyvern School returned sales £280, refund made by bank transfer
29 Jan	Sold goods on credit to Teme College, £2,495

Transactions for February

20-4

2 Feb	Sales £2,720, paid into bank
4 Feb	Paid rent on premises £500, by bank transfer
5 Feb	Purchased shop fittings £1,550, paid by bank transfer
10 Feb	Sales £3,995, paid into bank
12 Feb	Bank transfer, £7,500, to Tech Software
15 Feb	Purchased goods for resale £4,510, on credit from Tech Software
19 Feb	Bank transfer, £5,000, to Datasoft Limited
22 Feb	Sales £1,930, paid into bank
23 Feb	Teme College returned goods, £145
24 Feb	Sales £2,145, paid into bank
25 Feb	Purchased goods for resale £2,120, on credit from Associated Software
26 Feb	Sales £4,150, paid into bank

You are to:

(a) Record the January transactions in the books of account, and balance each account at 31 January 20-4.

(b) Draw up a trial balance at 31 January 20-4.

(c) Record the February transactions in the books of account, and balance each account at 28 February 20-4.

(d) Draw up a trial balance at 28 February 20-4.

Notes:

- Mark Tansall is not registered for Value Added Tax.

- Day books are not required.

- Mark Tansall's accounting system does not use control accounts.

- Make sure that you leave plenty of space for each account – particularly sales, purchases and bank.

4 Financial statements – the extended trial balance

Extended trial balance format

A blank photocopiable extended trial balance is included in the Appendix of *Financial Accounting: Preparing Financial Statements Tutorial*, and is also available in the Products and Resources section of www.osbornebooks.co.uk. It is advisable to enlarge it up to full A4 size. Alternatively you can set up a computer spreadsheet, but remember to allow for all the rows shown on the layout – they will be needed in later Workbook activities.

4.1 Which **one** of the following does not appear in the statement of profit or loss?

(a)	Closing inventory	
(b)	Purchases	
(c)	Interest paid	
(d)	Cash	

4.2 Which **one** of the following does not appear in the statement of financial position?

(a)	Closing inventory	
(b)	Sales revenue	
(c)	Trade receivables	
(d)	Bank	

4.3   The following trial balance has been extracted by Matt Smith at 31 December 20-3:

	Dr	Cr
	£	£
Opening inventory	14,350	
Purchases	114,472	
Sales revenue		259,688
Business rates	13,718	
Heating and lighting	12,540	
Wages and salaries	42,614	
Vehicle expenses	5,817	
Advertising	6,341	
Premises at cost	75,000	
Office equipment at cost	33,000	
Vehicles at cost	21,500	
Receivables ledger control	23,854	
Bank	1,235	
Cash	125	
Capital		62,500
Drawings	12,358	
Loan from bank		35,000
Payables ledger control		14,258
Value Added Tax		5,478
Closing inventory – statement of profit or loss		16,280
Closing inventory – statement of financial position	16,280	
	393,204	393,204

You are to prepare the extended trial balance of Matt Smith for the year ended 31 December 20-3.

4.4   The following trial balance has been extracted by Clare Lewis at 31 December 20-4:

	Dr	Cr
	£	£
Receivables ledger control	18,600	
Payables ledger control		11,480
Value Added Tax		1,870
Bank		4,610
Capital		25,250
Sales revenue		144,810
Purchases	96,318	
Opening inventory	16,010	
Salaries	18,465	
Heating and lighting	1,820	
Rent and rates	5,647	
Vehicles at cost	9,820	
Office equipment at cost	5,500	
Sundry expenses	845	
Vehicle expenses	1,684	
Drawings	13,311	
Closing inventory – statement of profit or loss		13,735
Closing inventory – statement of financial position	13,735	
	201,755	201,755

You are to prepare the extended trial balance of Clare Lewis for the year ended 31 December 20-4.

5 Accruals and prepayments

Extended trial balance format

A blank photocopiable extended trial balance is included in the Appendix of *Financial Accounting: Preparing Financial Statements Tutorial*, and is also available in the Products and Resources section of www.osbornebooks.co.uk. It is advisable to enlarge it up to full A4 size. Alternatively you can set up a computer spreadsheet, but remember to allow for all the rows shown on the layout – they will be needed in later Workbook activities.

5.1 A credit balance at the start of the year on an expenses account indicates:

(a)	A liability and an expense accrued	
(b)	An asset and an expense prepaid	
(c)	An asset and an expense accrued	
(d)	A liability and an expense prepaid	

5.2 Which **one** of the following is an asset?

(a)	Trade payables	
(b)	Wages accrued	
(c)	Bank overdraft	
(d)	Income accrued	

5.3 This Activity is about ledger accounting, including accruals and prepayments, and preparing a trial balance.

You are working on the accounts of a business for the year ended 31 March 20-2. In this Activity you can ignore VAT.

Business policy: accounting for accruals and prepayments
An entry is made into the income or expense account and an opposite entry into the relevant asset or liability account. In the following period, this entry is reversed.

You have the following information:

Balances as at:	1 April 20-1 £
Accrual for selling expenses	400
Prepayment for vehicle expenses	150

The bank summary for the year shows payments for selling expenses of £12,700. Included in this figure is £1,650 for the quarter ended 30 April 20-2.

(a) **You are to** prepare the selling expenses account for the year ended 31 March 20-2 and close it off by showing the transfer to the statement of profit or loss. Dates are not required.

Selling expenses

	£		£

The bank summary for the year shows payments for vehicle expenses of £7,200. In April 20-2, £280 was paid for vehicle expenses incurred in March 20-2.

(b) **You are to** prepare the vehicle expenses account for the year ended 31 March 20-2 and close it off by showing the transfer to the statement of profit or loss. Include dates.

Vehicle expenses

		£			£

You have the following extract of balances from the general ledger.

(c) **Using your answers** to (a) and (b), and the figures given below, enter amounts in the appropriate debit or credit column for the accounts shown. Do not enter zeros in unused column cells.

Extract from trial balance as at 31 March 20-2

Account	£	Dr £	Cr £
Accrued expenses			
Capital	45,000		
Discounts allowed	470		
Drawings	12,500		
Interest paid	380		
Office equipment at cost	24,500		
Prepaid expenses			
Purchases returns	2,740		

5.4 The following trial balance has been extracted by Cindy Hayward, who runs a delicatessen shop, at 30 June 20-4:

	Dr £	Cr £
Capital		90,932
Drawings	10,000	
Purchases	148,500	
Sales revenue		210,900
Repairs to buildings	848	
Vehicles at cost	15,000	
Vehicle expenses	1,540	
Land and buildings at cost	185,000	
Loan from bank		110,000
Bank	540	
Shop fittings at cost	12,560	
Wages	30,280	
Discounts allowed	135	
Discounts received		1,319
Rates and insurance	2,690	
Receivables ledger control	3,175	
Payables ledger control		8,295
Heating and lighting	3,164	
General expenses	4,680	
Sales returns	855	
Purchases returns		1,221
Opening inventory	6,210	
Value Added Tax		2,510
Closing inventory – statement of profit or loss		7,515
Closing inventory – statement of financial position	7,515	
	432,692	432,692

Notes at 30 June 20-4:

- Rates prepaid £255.

- Wages accrued £560.

- Vehicle expenses accrued £85.

- Goods costing £200 were taken by Cindy Hayward for her own use.

You are to prepare the extended trial balance of Cindy Hayward for the year ended 30 June 20-4.

6 Depreciation of non-current assets

Extended trial balance format

A blank photocopiable extended trial balance is included in the Appendix of *Financial Accounting: Preparing Financial Statements Tutorial*, and is also available in the Products and Resources section of www.osbornebooks.co.uk. It is advisable to enlarge it up to full A4 size. Alternatively you can set up a computer spreadsheet, but remember to allow for all the rows shown on the layout – they will be needed in later Workbook activities.

6.1 A car which cost £20,000 is being depreciated at 30% per year using the diminishing balance method. At the end of three years it will have a carrying amount of:

(a)	£2,000	
(b)	£6,860	
(c)	£13,140	
(d)	£18,000	

6.2 A car is being depreciated using the diminishing balance method. The original cost of the car was £15,000. At the end of year three it has a carrying amount of £5,145. What percentage of diminishing balance is being used?

(a)	20%	
(b)	25%	
(c)	30%	
(d)	35%	

6.3   A machine which originally cost £1,000 is sold for £350 (both amounts net of VAT). The machinery: accumulated depreciation account shows a balance of £620. This means that there is a:

(a)	Loss on disposal of £380	
(b)	Gain on disposal of £350	
(c)	Loss on disposal of £30	
(d)	Gain on disposal of £30	

6.4   The bookkeeping entries to record a gain on disposal of non-current assets are:

	Debit	Credit	
(a)	Non-current asset account	Statement of profit or loss	
(b)	Disposals account	Statement of profit or loss	
(c)	Statement of profit or loss	Disposals account	
(d)	Bank account	Statement of profit or loss	

6.5   This Activity is about recording non-current asset information in the general ledger.

- You are working on the accounts of a business that is registered for VAT.

- During the year an old machine was sold.

- The machine had been bought for £8,000 plus VAT (the VAT was reclaimed), as already shown in the machine at cost account.

- Two years' depreciation has been applied.

- Depreciation is provided at 20% per year on a diminishing balance basis.

- The machine was sold for £4,800 plus VAT (at 20%), with payment being received into the bank.

You are to:

(a) Calculate the accumulated depreciation on the machine now sold:

Year 1	£
Year 2	£
Total	£

(b) Make entries in the accounts which follow to record the disposal of the machine, showing clearly any balance carried down or transferred to the statement of profit or loss.

Machine at cost

Balance b/d	£8,000		

Machine: disposals

Bank

(c) Tick the relevant box to show whether there is a gain or loss on disposal of the machine.

gain	
loss	

6.6   The following trial balance has been extracted by the bookkeeper of Wintergreen Supplies at 31 December 20-6:

	Dr	Cr
	£	£
Premises at cost	120,000	
Premises: accumulated depreciation		7,200
Bank loan		52,800
Capital		70,000
Receivables ledger control	11,900	
Payables ledger control		11,500
Drawings	6,750	
Cash	150	
Opening inventory	4,200	
Office equipment at cost	5,000	
Office equipment: accumulated depreciation		1,000
Vehicles at cost	10,000	
Vehicles: accumulated depreciation		2,000
Bank		750
Sales revenue		194,850
Purchases	154,000	
Wages	20,500	
Sundry expenses	9,500	
Value Added Tax		1,750
Disposal of non-current asset		150
Closing inventory – statement of profit or loss		5,200
Closing inventory – statement of financial position	5,200	
	347,200	347,200

Notes at 31 December 20-6:

*   Depreciate premises at 2% using the straight-line method.

*   Depreciate vehicles and office equipment at 20% using the straight-line method.

*   Wages prepaid are £560, and sundry expenses accrued are £500.

You are to prepare the extended trial balance of Wintergreen Supplies for the year ended 31 December 20-6.

7 Irrecoverable debts and allowance for doubtful receivables

Extended trial balance format

A blank photocopiable extended trial balance is included in the Appendix of *Financial Accounting: Preparing Financial Statements Tutorial*, and is also available in the Products and Resources section of www.osbornebooks.co.uk. It is advisable to enlarge it up to full A4 size. Alternatively you can set up a computer spreadsheet, but remember to allow for all the rows shown on the layout – they will be needed in later Workbook activities.

7.1 The accounts supervisor of the firm where you work has instructed you to write off the trade receivable account of T Neal as irrecoverable. Which one of the following entries will you make in the double-entry accounts? (Assume that the business does not use control accounts.)

	Debit	Credit	
(a)	T Neal's account	Irrecoverable debts account	
(b)	Bank account	T Neal's account	
(c)	Irrecoverable debts account	T Neal's account	
(d)	T Neal's account	Allowance for doubtful receivables account	

Note: ignore VAT.

7.2 An increase in the allowance for doubtful receivables will:

(a)	Decrease profit for the year	
(b)	Be recorded in the trade receivables accounts in receivables ledger	
(c)	Decrease the bank balance	
(d)	Increase profit for the year	

7.3   The statement of profit or loss of a business has been prepared showing a loss for the year of £2,350. A reduction of £150 in the allowance for doubtful receivables should have been made, and irrecoverable debts of £70 should have been written off. Loss for the year will now be:

(a)	£2,130	
(b)	£2,270	
(c)	£2,430	
(d)	£2,570	

Note: ignore VAT.

7.4 You are the bookkeeper at Enterprise Trading Company. The following information is available for the financial years ending 31 December 20-5, 20-6, 20-7:

	£
• Trade receivables balances at 31 December 20-5, before writing off irrecoverable debts	105,200
• Irrecoverable debts written off on 31 December 20-5	1,800
• 2.5% allowance for doubtful receivables created at 31 December 20-5	
• Trade receivables balances at 31 December 20-6, before writing off irrecoverable debts	115,600
• Irrecoverable debts written off on 31 December 20-6	2,400
• 2.5% allowance for doubtful receivables adjusted in line with the change in the level of trade receivables at 31 December 20-6	
• Trade receivables balances at 31 December 20-7, before writing off irrecoverable debts	110,200
• Irrecoverable debts written off on 31 December 20-7	1,400
• 2.5% allowance for doubtful receivables adjusted in line with the change in the level of trade receivables at 31 December 20-7	

Note: ignore VAT.

You are to show the effect of the above transactions on the financial statements in the following table:

Year	Statement of profit or loss			Statement of financial position	
	Dr Irrecoverable debts £	Dr Allowance for doubtful receivables: adjustment £	Cr Allowance for doubtful receivables: adjustment £	Dr Receivables ledger control £	Cr Allowance for doubtful receivables £
20-5					
20-6					
20-7					

7.5   This Activity is about accounting for irrecoverable debts and allowance for doubtful receivables and preparing a trial balance.

You are working on the financial statements of a business for the year ended 31 December 20-6. In this task you can ignore VAT.

You have the following information:

Irrecoverable debts to be written off:	£
Craven Traders	75
Harris and Co	110
P Mahon	55
Allowance for doubtful receivables at 1 January 20-6	300

The balance of trade receivables (receivables ledger control account) before irrecoverable debts are written off is £12,740. The allowance for doubtful receivables is to be 2% of trade receivables after irrecoverable debts.

(a)   **You are to** prepare the irrecoverable debts account for the year ended 31 December 20-6 and close it off by showing the transfer to the statement of profit or loss. Dates are not required.

Irrecoverable debts

	£		£

(b) **You are to** prepare the allowance for doubtful receivables account for the year ended 31 December 20-6 and to show clearly the balance carried down. Include dates.

Allowance for doubtful receivables

		£			£

You have the following extract of balances from the general ledger.

(c) **Using your answers** from **(a)** and **(b)**, record the adjustments on the extract from the extended trial balance. Do not enter zeros in unused column cells.

Extract from trial balance as at 31 December 20-6

Account	Ledger balances		Adjustments	
	Dr £	Cr £	Dr £	Cr £
Allowance for doubtful receivables		300		
Allowance for doubtful receivables: adjustment				
Irrecoverable debts				
Payables ledger control		8,960		
Receivables ledger control	12,740			
Vehicles at cost	20,000			
Vehicles: accumulated depreciation		11,200		
Wages	22,850			

7.6 The following trial balance has been extracted by the bookkeeper of Jane Jones, who sells carpets, as at 31 December 20-5:

	Dr	Cr
	£	£
Receivables ledger control	37,200	
Payables ledger control		30,640
Value Added Tax		4,280
Bank	14,640	
Capital		50,500
Sales revenue		289,620
Purchases	182,636	
Opening inventory	32,020	
Wages and salaries	36,930	
Heat and light	3,640	
Rent and rates	11,294	
Vehicles at cost	20,000	
Vehicles: accumulated depreciation		4,000
Machinery at cost	10,000	
Machinery: accumulated depreciation		1,000
Sundry expenses	1,690	
Vehicle expenses	3,368	
Drawings	26,622	
Closing inventory – statement of profit or loss		34,000
Closing inventory – statement of financial position	34,000	
	414,040	414,040

Notes at 31 December 20-5:

- Irrecoverable debts of £2,200 are to be written off (ignore VAT) and an allowance for doubtful receivables of 5% is to be created.

- Depreciate vehicles at 20% per annum and machinery at 10% per annum, using the diminishing balance method.

- There are sundry expenses accrued of £270, and rates prepaid of £2,190.

You are to prepare the extended trial balance of Jane Jones for the year ended 31 December 20-5.

8 Framework of accounting

8.1 For the following three primary users of financial statements, identify how they might use the information contained in the statements:

User	Use of information
HM Revenue & Customs	
Bank	
Potential investor	

8.2 Link the boxes on the left with lines to match the uses of financial records and statements with the most likely reason for their use.

Uses	Reason
Internal control	To provide lenders with the current financial position
Measuring business performance	To ensure that financial records are accurate
Obtaining credit/financing	To provide information for tax and other purposes when required to do so
Statutory requirements	To compare financial reports and statements

8.3   Write a brief explanation of the following accounting principles (concepts):

Accounting principle	Explanation
Business entity	
Going concern	
Prudence	

8.4   A business matches income and expenses so that they relate to the same goods or services and the same accounting period.

Of the following accounting principles, which **one** best describes this rule of accounting?

(a)	Accruals	
(b)	Money measurement	
(c)	Going concern	
(d)	Materiality	

8.5 Link each of the boxes on the left with a line to match the fundamental qualitative accounting characteristics that most accurately describes the reason for its use.

Characteristic	Reason

Characteristic

Relevance

Faithful representation

Reason

Financial statements can be compared with those from previous years

Financial information is useful to financial users of statements

Users of financial information receive information in time to make decisions

Financial information must correspond to the effect of transactions or events

8.6 The International Financial Reporting Standards Framework for Financial Reporting identifies four enhancing qualitative characteristics that make financial information useful.

Under which **one** of the following are users presented with financial information clearly and concisely?

(a)	Timeliness	
(b)	Comparability	
(c)	Verifiability	
(d)	Understandability	

8.7 **(a)** With reference to financial statements, what is the significance of the word 'material' in material misstatements?

(b) Complete the following sentences by filling in the missing word – choose from: overstated, understated, overvalued, undervalued (each word may be used more than once):

(1) If profit is [ ] investors may be encouraged to buy a stake in the business.

(2) If profit is [ ] HM Revenue & Customs will receive a lower amount of tax than should be paid.

(3) If sales revenue is [ ] HM Revenue & Customs will receive a lower amount of VAT than should be paid.

(4) If assets are [ ] a lender may find that security for a loan is less than expected.

8.8 Link the boxes on the left with lines to match the ethical principles with the most likely application of the principles.

Principle	**Application**
Confidentiality	The accountant is not influenced by the owner(s) to manipulate profits
Objectivity	The accountant is up-to-date with current accounting standards and legal developments
Professional competence and due care	Financial statements should not contain false or misleading figures or statements
Integrity	Information from the financial statements is only discussed with those entitled to know

8.9 Write a description of professional scepticism, highlighting its characteristics.

8.10 **(a)** IAS 2 *Inventories* states that inventories are to be valued at [_____]

[_____]. (Complete the sentence.)

(b) A business buys twenty units of a product in January at a cost of £3.00 each; it buys ten more in February at £3.50 each, and ten in April at £4.00 each. Eight units are sold in March, and sixteen are sold in May.

What is the value of the closing inventory at the end of May using FIFO (first in, first out)?

FIFO	
£54	
£61	
£60	
£48	
£40	
£135	

8.11   YZ Limited is formed on 1 January 20-4 and trades in two products, Y and Z. At the end of its first half year, the inventory movements of the two products are as follows:

20-4	PRODUCT Y		PRODUCT Z	
	Bought *(units)*	**Sold** *(units)*	**Bought** *(units)*	**Sold** *(units)*
January	100 at £4.00		200 at £10.00	
February		80 at £10.00	100 at £9.50	
March	140 at £4.20			240 at £16.00
April	100 at £3.80		100 at £10.50	
May		140 at £10.00	140 at £10.00	
June	80 at £4.50			100 at £16.00

The company values inventory on the FIFO (first in, first out) method.

At 30 June 20-4, the net realisable value of each type of inventory is:

product Y	£1,750.00
product Z	£1,950.00
	————
	£3,700.00

You are to calculate the value of:

(a)   Sales revenue for the half year.

(b)   Closing inventory valuation at 30 June 20-4 for each product using the FIFO basis.

(c)   Amount at which the company's inventories should be valued on 30 June 20-4 in order to comply with IAS 2 *Inventories*.

(d)   Cost of sales for the half year in order to comply with IAS 2 *Inventories*.

8.12   A shop is valuing its inventory at the financial year-end. The following information is available:

•   Inventory at selling prices is £240,000.

•   The sales margin is 40%.

What is the cost price of inventory for the shop's financial statements?

£ [   ]

8.13 A business is valuing its inventory at the financial year-end. The following information is available:

- Inventory including VAT is £288,000.

- VAT is 20%.

What is the cost price of inventory for the business's financial statements?

£ [   ]

8.14 On 31 December 20-6 closing inventory has been valued at £25,000.

You are to complete the journal below to show the entries which will be made in the ledger accounts.

Journal

Date	Details	Reference	Dr	Cr
			£	£

9 Accounting for capital transactions

9.1   Which **one** of the following is an intangible non-current asset?

(a)	Vehicles	
(b)	Goodwill	
(c)	Hire purchase	
(d)	Premises	

9.2   Which **one** of the following is revenue expenditure?

(a)	Purchase of a computer for the office	
(b)	Legal costs for the purchase of property	
(c)	Cost of extension to property	
(d)	Quarterly electricity bill	

9.3   Which **one** of the following is capital expenditure?

(a)	Repairs to vehicles	
(b)	Goods taken by owner for own use	
(c)	Cost of materials used to extend the premises	
(d)	Renewing the electrical wiring in the office	

9.4   Wages paid to own employees who have redecorated the office are:

(a)	Capital expenditure	
(b)	Debited to the statement of profit or loss	
(c)	Debited to premises account	
(d)	Credited to the statement of profit or loss	

9.5 Classify the following costs:

		Capital expenditure	Revenue expenditure
(a)	Purchase of vehicles		
(b)	Depreciation of vehicles		
(c)	Rent paid on premises		
(d)	Wages and salaries		
(e)	Legal fees relating to the purchase of property		
(f)	Redecoration of office		
(g)	Installation of air-conditioning in office		
(h)	Wages of own employees used to build extension to the office		
(i)	Installation and setting up of a new machine		

9.6 John and Sara Smith run a delivery company called 'J & S Transport'. They started in business on 1 January 20-2 with two vans which cost £16,000 each (paid from the bank). On 1 January 20-4, a further two vans were bought at a cost of £18,000 each (paid from the bank) and, on 20 March 20-4, one of the original vans was sold for £8,000 (paid into the bank).

Depreciation is charged at 25% each year, using the diminishing balance method; depreciation is charged in the year of purchase, but not in the year of disposal.

The Smiths' financial year-end is 31 December.

You are to show the accounting entries (journal and cash book not required) to record the acquisition, depreciation and disposal of vans for the years 20-2, 20-3 and 20-4.

Notes:

- VAT is to be ignored.

- Use one non-current asset vehicles account for all vans, one depreciation charge account and one vehicles: accumulated depreciation account.

9.7   This Activity is about non-current assets. You are working for a business known as Marston Metals. Marston Metals is registered for VAT and has a financial year-end of 31 March.

The following is an extract from a purchase invoice received by Marston Metals:

To: Marston Metals Unit 10, Sunnydale Estate Marston MR3 8JK	Invoice 4728 Machine Supplies plc Wyvern Road Eveshore EV2 1QL		Date: 17 June 20-5
Pressing machine	Reference AB347	1	2,500.00
Installation of machine		1	160.00
One year service contract		1	100.00
VAT @ 20%			552.00
Total			3,312.00
Settlement terms: strictly 30 days net			

Marston Metals paid the invoice in full on 30 June 20-5.

The following information relates to the sale of a van:

Registration number	AB69 TPJ
Date of sale	14 February 20-6
Selling price	£8,000.00

- Marston Metals has a policy of capitalising expenditure over £500.

- Vehicles are depreciated at 25% on a diminishing balance basis.

- Machinery is depreciated at 20% on a straight-line basis assuming no residual value.

- Non-current assets are depreciated in the year of acquisition but not in the year of disposal.

Record the following information in the extract from the non-current asset register on the next page.

- Any acquisitions of non-current assets during the year ended 31 March 20-6.

- Any disposals of non-current assets during the year ended 31 March 20-6.

- Depreciation for the year ended 31 March 20-6.

EXTRACT FROM NON-CURRENT ASSET REGISTER							
Description/serial no	Acquisition date	Cost £	Depreciation charges £	Carrying amount £	Funding method	Disposal proceeds £	Disposal date
Machinery							
Moulding machine	12/08/-3	10,000.00			Cash		
Year end 31/03/-4			2,000.00	8,000.00			
Year end 31/03/-5			2,000.00	6,000.00			
Year end 31/03/-6							
Year end 31/03/-6							
Vehicles							
AB69 TPJ	11/06/-3	16,400.00			Cash		
Year end 31/03/-4			4,100.00	12,300.00			
Year end 31/03/-5			3,075.00	9,225.00			
Year end 31/03/-6							
AB75 PZE	01/01/-5	15,200.00			Part-exchange		
Year end 31/03/-5			3,800.00	11,400.00			
Year end 31/03/-6							

9.8   You are working on the accounts of Ailsa's business.

A non-current asset has been wrongly classified as a current asset. What is the effect on the following items in the financial statements?

Item	Understated	Overstated	No effect
Net profit			
Current assets			
Current liabilities			
Non-current assets			

10   Control accounts

10.1   Indicate whether the following errors would cause a difference between the balance of the receivables ledger control account and the total of the balances in the receivables ledger.

Error		Difference	No difference
(a)	Sales returns day book was undercast by £100		
(b)	A credit note for £75 was credited to the account of Martley Traders instead of Martley Manufacturing – both are receivables ledger accounts		
(c)	The receivables ledger account of C Fernandez, £125, has been written off as irrecoverable, but no entry has been made in receivables ledger control account		
(d)	A set-off entry for £45 has been incorrectly recorded as £54 in the receivables ledger control account and in the receivables ledger account		

10.2 On 31 December 20-6 the balances of the trade payables accounts in the payables ledger of Thomas Limited were listed, totalled, and compared with the balance of the payables ledger control account. The total of the list of payables ledger balances amounted to £55,946. Investigations were carried out and the following errors were discovered:

(a) A payables ledger balance of £553 had been listed as £535.

(b) Discounts received of £100 had been credited to the trade payables account.

(c) A credit note received for £141 had not been recorded in the trade payables account.

(d) A payables ledger balance of £225 had been listed twice.

You are to record the appropriate adjustments in the table below; show clearly the amount involved and whether it is to be added or subtracted.

		£
Total of list of payables ledger balances		55,946
Adjustment for (a)	add/subtract	....
Adjustment for (b)	add/subtract	....
Adjustment for (c)	add/subtract	....
Adjustment for (d)	add/subtract	....
Revised total to agree with payables ledger control account		....

10.3 Prepare a VAT control account for the month of January 20-1 from the following information:

20-1		£
1 Jan	Credit balance b/d	6,240
31 Jan	VAT on purchases	11,046
31 Jan	VAT on purchases returns	498
31 Jan	VAT on discounts received	164
31 Jan	VAT on credit sales	19,047
31 Jan	VAT on sales returns	722
31 Jan	VAT on non-current assets purchased	1,845
31 Jan	Bank payment to HM Revenue & Customs	6,240

Balance the account at 31 January 20-1.

10.4 Prepare a wages and salaries control account for the month of February 20-2 from the following information:

		£
•	Wages expenses	17,342
•	Bank payments to employees	11,367
•	Pension fund liability	2,025
•	Trade union fees liability	295

The liability to HM Revenue & Customs for the month is to be entered as the balancing figure.

10.5 This Activity is about preparing reconciliations.

The receivables ledger has been compared with receivables ledger control account at 31 March and the following points noted:

1 £120 of discounts allowed to trade receivables and entered in their receivables ledger accounts has not been entered in receivables ledger control account.

2 A set-off entry for £220 has been credited to the receivables ledger account of Barker Limited instead of to the receivables ledger account of Baker Limited.

3 In the cash book, the column for receipts from trade receivables has been undercast (underadded) by £100.

4 The account of D Doherty, £95, has been written off as irrecoverable in receivables ledger, but has not been recorded in receivables ledger control account.

5 A credit sale of £580 has been debited to the receivables ledger account of Crossjoint Limited instead of to the receivables ledger account of Crossways Limited.

6 A Faster Payment receipt from a credit customer for £745 for a debt outstanding at 31 March was received in April.

The total of the account balances in receivables ledger is £24,275 debit and the balance of receivables ledger control account is £24,590 debit.

Use the following table to show the **three** items that should appear in the receivables ledger control account. Enter only **one** figure for each line. Do not enter zeros in unused cells.

Adjustment number	Debit £	Credit £

10.6 This Activity is about preparing reconciliations.

The payables ledger has been compared with payables ledger control account at 31 March and the following points noted:

1   The total column of purchases day book has been undercast (underadded) by £500.

2   A set-off entry for £190 has been omitted from payables ledger control account.

3   A purchases return of £240 has been debited to the payables ledger account of Spence Limited instead of the payables ledger account of Spencer Limited.

4   £140 of discounts received from trade payables has been entered on the wrong side of payables ledger control account.

5   A Faster Payment of £759 was sent to a credit supplier, but the amount that should have been paid is £795.

6   A Faster Payment to a credit customer for £1,054 was due on 31 March, but the payment was made in April.

The total of the account balances in payables ledger is £18,790 credit and the balance of payables ledger control account is £18,760 credit.

Use the following table to show the **three** items that should appear in the payables ledger control account. Enter only **one** figure for each line. Do not enter zeros in unused cells.

Adjustment number	Debit £	Credit £

10.7   This Activity is about preparing reconciliations.

The bank statement has been compared with the bank columns of the cash book at 31 March and the following points noted:

1   A cheque for £1,210 paid into the bank yesterday is not shown on the bank statement.

2   A direct debit payment made by the bank for £360 has not been entered in the cash book.

3   A BACS receipt from a customer for £230 has been incorrectly entered in the cash book as £320.

4   Bank charges and interest of £120 have not been entered in the cash book.

5   A Faster Payment receipt from a customer for £258 for a debt outstanding at 31 March was received in April.

6   The bank made an error. On the last day of the month, a payment of £950 on the statement was duplicated.

The balance showing on the bank statement is a credit of £1,810 and the balance in the cash book is a debit of £4,540.

Use the following table to show the **three** items that should appear on the cash book side of the reconciliation. Enter only **one** figure for each line. Do not enter zeros in unused cells.

Adjustment number	Debit £	Credit £

10.8   This Activity is about preparing reconciliations.

Ella has received her bank statement for the month of April 20-2 and has asked you to complete the bank reconciliation statement. At 30 April 20-2:

- her bank statement shows a balance of money in the bank of £546.24 credit
- her cash book shows a debit balance of £419.68

The following items are outstanding on either the bank statement or the cash book:

- Bank charges of £15 are on the bank statement but not in the cash book.
- A bank receipt for £125.98 from Oxley Ltd is on the bank statement but not in the cash book.
- A cheque for £260.75 from Groves & Co, which was paid into the bank yesterday, has been entered in the cash book but is not shown on the bank statement.
- A payment for £276.33 by cheque from Ella to Stanton Ltd has been entered in the cash book but is not shown on the bank statement.

(a)   What is the amended cash book balance at 30 April 20-2 after dealing with the items? Indicate whether it is debit or credit.

£ | | debit | credit |
|---|---|---|

(b)   Complete a bank reconciliation statement as at 30 April 20-2.

Select your entries from the following list: Bank charges, Groves & Co, Oxley Ltd, Stanton Ltd.

Bank reconciliation statement as at 30 April 20-2	£
Closing bank statement balance	
Less unpresented cheques	
Add outstanding lodgements	
Closing cash book balance	

The journal and correction of errors

11.1 Which **one** of the following will not be recorded in the journal?

(a)	An irrecoverable debt written off	
(b)	Correction of an error of omission	
(c)	Closing inventory valuation at the year-end	
(d)	Bank payment to a trade payable	

11.2 The purchase of stationery, £25, has been debited in error to office equipment account. Which **one** of the following journal entries will correct the error?

	Debit		**Credit**		
(a)	Office equipment	£25	Stationery	£25	
(b)	Suspense	£25	Office equipment	£25	
(c)	Stationery	£25	Office equipment	£25	
(d)	Stationery	£25	Suspense	£25	

Note: ignore VAT.

11.3 A trial balance fails to agree by £27 and the difference is placed to a suspense account. Later it is found that a payment for vehicle repairs of £63 has been entered in the vehicle repairs account as £36. Which **one** of the following journal entries will correct the error?

	Debit		**Credit**		
(a)	Suspense Vehicle repairs	£36 £63	Vehicle repairs Suspense	£36 £63	
(b)	Suspense	£27	Vehicle repairs	£27	
(c)	Vehicle repairs	£27	Bank	£27	
(d)	Vehicle repairs Suspense	£36 £63	Suspense Vehicle repairs	£36 £63	

Note: ignore VAT.

11.4 What is the effect on the previously reported profit for the year of making adjustments for the following errors?

		Profit increases	Profit decreases
(a)	Sales account overcast		
(b)	Closing inventory undervalued		
(c)	Telephone expenses account undercast		
(d)	Discounts received omitted		
(e)	Depreciation charges for vehicles omitted		
(f)	Irrecoverable debt not written off		
(g)	Decrease in allowance for doubtful receivables not made		

11.5 This Activity is about recording journal entries.

You are working on the financial statements of a business with a year-end of 31 March. A trial balance has been drawn up and a suspense account opened with a debit balance of £5,840. You now need to make some corrections and adjustments for the year ended 31 March 20-2.

Record the journal entries needed in the general ledger to deal with the items below. You should:

- Remove any incorrect entries, where appropriate

- Post the correct entries

You do not need to give narratives.

Do NOT enter zeros into unused column cells.

Ignore VAT.

(a) Entries need to be made for an irrecoverable debt of £300.

Journal

	Dr £	Cr £

(b) A purchase of office equipment for £4,000 has been made from the bank. The correct entry was made to the bank account, but no other entries were made.

Journal

	Dr £	Cr £

(c) No entries have been made for closing inventory for the year-end 31 March 20-2. Closing inventory has been valued at cost at £18,380. Included in this figure are some items costing £940 that will be sold for £700.

Journal

	Dr £	Cr £

(d) The figures from the columns of the purchases day book for 31 March have been totalled correctly as follows:

Purchases column	£4,600
VAT column	£920
Total column	£5,520

The amounts have been recorded in the accounts as follows:

Dr Purchases	£4,600
Cr VAT	£920
Cr Payables ledger control	£5,520

Journal

	Dr £	Cr £

11.6 This Activity is about completing an extended balance.

You have the following extended trial balance. The adjustments have already been correctly entered.

Extend the figures into the statement of profit or loss and statement of financial position.

Do NOT enter zeros into unused column cells.

Make the columns balance by entering figures in the correct places.

Extended trial balance

Ledger account	Ledger balances		Adjustments		Statement of profit or loss		Statement of financial position	
	Dr £	Cr £	Dr £	Cr £	Dr £	Cr £	Dr £	Cr £
Allowance for doubtful receivables		1,200	100					1,100
Allowance for doubtful receivables adjustment				100		100		
Bank	15,300						15,300	
Capital		30,000						30,000
Closing inventory			25,230	25,230		25,230	25,230	
Depreciation charges			2,500		2,500			
Office equipment at cost	20,000						20,000	
Office equipment: accumulated depreciation		8,500		2,500				11,000
Office expenses	12,700		500		13,200			
Opening inventory	22,680				22,680			
Payroll expenses	25,920			350	25,570			
Purchases	85,500		400		85,900			
Payables ledger control		25,270						25,270
Rent and rates	5,400			250	5,150			
Sales		151,200				151,200		
Receivables ledger control	30,380						30,380	
Suspense	300		600	900				
VAT		2,010						2,010
Profit/loss for the year					21,530			21,530
	218,180	218,180	29,330	29,330	176,530	176,530	90,910	90,910

11.7 The trial balance for Anya's business has been produced for the year ended 31 December 20-5. The debit column totals £121,135 and the credit column totals £121,340.

The following errors and omissions have been found and you, as the accounts assistant, have been asked to correct them. Use the journal layout below. Dates and narratives are not required. Errors and omissions:

- The closing inventory has not been recorded in the accounts. It is valued at £9,180.

- Additional capital of £2,500 paid into the bank account by Anya has been recorded in the correct accounts but on the incorrect side of each account.

- The balance of discounts received account, £650, has been calculated wrongly and should be £560.

- A bank payment for stationery of £138 (including VAT) has been correctly recorded in the bank and VAT accounts but has not been recorded in the stationery account.

Tutorial note: where appropriate, use a single journal entry (one debit, one credit) rather than two entries.

Select your account names from the following list: Bank, Capital, Closing inventory: sfp*, Closing inventory: spl**, Discounts received, Inventory, Stationery, Suspense.

*   statement of financial position

**   statement of profit or loss

Journal number: 278	31 December 20-5	
Account name	**Debit**	**Credit**
	£	£

12 Preparing financial statements

12.1 Cost of sales is calculated as:

(a)	Opening inventory + purchases – closing inventory	
(b)	Purchases – opening inventory + closing inventory	
(c)	Opening inventory + purchases + closing inventory	
(d)	Purchases – opening inventory – closing inventory	

12.2 Which **one** of the following is used to calculate profit for the year?

(a)	Two-column trial balance	
(b)	Receivables ledger	
(c)	Statement of financial position	
(d)	Statement of profit or loss	

12.3 Which **one** of the following describes net current assets?

(a)	The excess of non-current assets over non-current liabilities	
(b)	The excess of current assets over non-current liabilities	
(c)	The excess of current assets over current liabilities	
(d)	The excess of non-current assets over current liabilities	

12.4   **You are to** fill in the missing figures for the following sole trader businesses:

	Sales	Opening inventory	Purchases	Closing inventory	Gross profit	Expenses	Profit/loss* for year
	£	£	£	£	£	£	£
Business A	20,000	5,000	10,000	3,000	....	4,000	....
Business B	35,000	8,000	15,000	5,000	....	....	10,000
Business C	....	6,500	18,750	7,250	18,500	11,750	....
Business D	45,250	9,500	....	10,500	20,750	....	10,950
Business E	71,250	....	49,250	9,100	22,750	24,450	....
Business F	25,650	4,950	13,750	....	11,550	....	−3,450

*Note: a loss is indicated by a minus sign.

12.5 You have the following information about a sole trader business. The value of assets and liabilities as at 1 April 20-1 was:

•	Inventory	£14,270
•	Bank (overdrawn)	£3,210
•	Trade payables	£6,180
•	Non-current assets at carrying amount	£25,500
•	Bank loan	£12,500
•	Trade receivables	£9,450

There were no other assets or liabilities.

(a) Calculate the following as at 1 April 20-1. Do NOT enter any figures as negative.

Assets   £ [   ]

Liabilities £ [   ]

Capital   £ [   ]

(b) Which of the following best describes goodwill? Tick **one** answer

(a)	A liability, where payment is due in more than one year's time	
(b)	An intangible non-current asset which does not have material substance	
(c)	A short-term asset which changes regularly	
(d)	A tangible non-current asset which has material substance	

12.6 This Activity is about calculating missing balances and the accounting equation.

You are given the following information about a sole trader as at 1 April 20-4:

The value of assets and liabilities was:

- Non-current assets at carrying amount   £35,400
- Inventory   £12,200
- Trade receivables   £21,650
- Bank (overdrawn)   £3,240
- Trade payables   £12,790

There were no other assets or liabilities.

(a) Calculate the capital account balance as at 1 April 20-4.

£ [   ]

(b) On 30 April 20-4, a new machine is purchased for use in the business and is paid for immediately by bank payment. Tick the boxes to show what effect this transaction will have on the balances. You must choose **one** answer for **each** line.

	Debit	**Credit**	**No change**
Non-current assets			
Trade receivables			
Trade payables			
Bank			
Capital			

(c) Which of the following is best described as a non-current liability? Tick **one** answer.

(a)	A bank loan repayable in two years' time	
(b)	A bank overdraft	
(c)	Trade payables	
(d)	Trade receivables	

12.7 The following trial balance has been extracted by Lucy Chazal at 31 December 20-4:

	Dr	Cr
	£	£
Opening inventory	32,147	
Purchases	201,318	
Sales revenue		397,242
Business rates	18,210	
Heating and lighting	23,680	
Payroll expenses	77,211	
Vehicle expenses	7,619	
Advertising	15,483	
Premises at cost	150,000	
Office equipment at cost	25,000	
Vehicles at cost	32,500	
Receivables ledger control	33,482	
Bank	2,704	
Cash	525	
Capital		148,500
Drawings	27,212	
Loan from bank		60,000
Payables ledger control		35,138
Value Added Tax		6,211
Closing inventory: statement of profit or loss		35,419
Closing inventory: statement of financial position	35,419	
	682,510	682,510

You are to prepare the financial statements of Lucy Chazal for the year ended 31 December 20-4, using the conventional format.

12.8   An extract from the trial balance of Lisa James is as follows:

Trial balance (extract) as at 31 March 20-7		
	Dr	Cr
	£	£
Opening inventory	17,540	
Sales revenue		127,500
Purchases	77,200	
Sales returns	2,150	
Purchases returns		3,040
Carriage in	600	
Carriage out	1,540	
Discounts received		230
Discounts allowed	470	
Other expenses	35,830	
Closing inventory: statement of profit or loss		19,960

You are to prepare the statement of profit or loss of Lisa James for the year ended 31 March 20-7, using the conventional format.

12.9   This Activity is about financial statements.

Identify whether each of the following transactions would lead to an increase in, a decrease in, or have no effect on the owner's capital:

Transaction	Increase	Decrease	No effect
New non-current assets paid for from the business bank account			
Owner's computer transferred into the business			
Loss for the year			
Owner's drawings			
Owner arranges a bank overdraft for the business			

12.10 This Activity is about financial statements.

Identify whether the following statements are true or false:

Statement	True	False
The owner's drawings account has a debit balance		
Net current assets is current assets plus current liabilities		
Trade payables is a current asset		
A bank overdraft is a current liability		
Profit for the year is gross profit plus expenses		
Cost of sales is opening inventory plus purchases minus closing inventory		

13 Sole trader financial statements

13.1   A statement of profit or loss shows a profit for the year of £14,900. It is discovered that no allowance has been made for advertising expenses accrued of £620 and rent prepaid of £450 at the year-end. What is the adjusted profit for the year?

(a)	£14,730	
(b)	£15,070	
(c)	£15,970	
(d)	£13,830	

13.2   Identify whether the following items will be stated in the year-end statement of profit or loss as income or expense by putting a tick in the relevant column of the table below.

Item	Income	Expense
Gain on disposal of non-current asset		
Decrease in allowance for doubtful receivables		
Irrecoverable debts		
Discounts allowed		
Depreciation charges		
Commission received		

13.3   A statement of profit or loss shows a profit for the year of £18,790. The owner of the business wishes to increase the allowance for doubtful receivables by £800 and to write off irrecoverable debts of £250. What is the adjusted profit for the year?

(a)	£18,240	
(b)	£19,840	
(c)	£19,340	
(d)	£17,740	

13.4   You have the following trial balance for a sole trader known as Tysoe Trading. All the necessary year-end adjustments have been made.

(a)   Prepare a statement of profit or loss (on the next page) for the business for the year ended 31 March 20-6.

Tysoe Trading
Trial balance as at 31 March 20-6

	Dr	Cr
	£	£
Accruals		460
Bank	4,610	
Capital		35,500
Closing inventory	10,200	10,200
Depreciation charges	2,500	
Discounts allowed	490	
Drawings	10,300	
General expenses	25,720	
Office equipment at cost	20,400	
Office equipment: accumulated depreciation		6,500
Opening inventory	11,450	
Payroll expenses	29,610	
Prepayments	990	
Purchases	64,330	
Payables ledger control		10,310
Receivables ledger control	18,920	
Rent and rates	7,240	
Sales revenue		140,680
Value Added Tax		3,110
	206,760	206,760

Tysoe Trading		
Statement of profit or loss for the year ended 31 March 20-6		
	£	£
Sales revenue		
Cost of sales		
Gross profit		
Less expenses:		
Total expenses		
Profit/loss for the year		

(b) Indicate where accruals of expenses should be shown in the statement of financial position.
Tick **one** from:

(a)	As a non-current asset	
(b)	As a current asset	
(c)	As a current liability	
(d)	As an addition to capital	

(c) State the meaning of a credit balance for disposal of a non-current asset in a trial balance. Tick **one** from:

(a)	The business has made a gain on disposal	
(b)	The business has made a loss on disposal	
(c)	The asset has been under depreciated	
(d)	The asset has been part-exchanged on disposal	

13.5 The following adjusted trial balance has been taken from the books of Rhianna Aitken, who sells kitchenware, as at 31 March 20-1:

	Dr £	Cr £
Receivables ledger control	4,110	
Allowance for doubtful receivables		880
Allowance for doubtful receivables: adjustment	220	
Payables ledger control		11,490
Value Added Tax		1,720
Bank		2,360
Capital		27,500
Sales revenue		166,240
Purchases	85,330	
Opening inventory	18,890	
Shop wages	35,560	
Prepayment of shop wages	440	
Heat and light	2,680	
Rent and rates	10,570	
Accrual of rent and rates		590
Shop fittings at cost	36,000	
Depreciation charges	4,750	
Shop fittings: accumulated depreciation		12,380
Disposal of non-current asset		600
Irrecoverable debts	150	
Drawings	25,060	
Closing inventory	22,450	22,450
	246,210	246,210

You are to prepare the financial statements of Rhianna Aitken for the year ended 31 March 20-1, using the conventional format.

13.6 You are preparing the accounting records of Nishan's business. You have the following information about Nishan's capital account for the year:

- Capital account balance at start of year was £55,200 credit.

- Profit for the year was £18,750.

- Cash drawings were £10,330.

- Goods taken for his own use by Nishan were £1,270.

- Nishan paid £5,000 into the bank to increase his capital.

- Nishan put his computer into the business at a valuation of £1,000.

You are to prepare Nishan's capital account for the year and to show the balance c/d.

Select your account names from the following list: Balance b/d, Balance c/d, Bank, Capital, Computer, Drawings, Statement of financial position, Statement of profit or loss.

Capital			
Account name	**£**	**Account name**	**£**
Total		Total	

14   Partnership financial statements

14.1   A partnership may choose to over-ride some or all of the accounting rules in the Partnership Act 1890 by the partners entering into a separate:

(a)	Appropriation account	
(b)	Accounting policy	
(c)	Partnership agreement	
(d)	Loan agreement	

14.2   Profits of a two-person partnership are £32,100 before the following are taken into account:

- interest on partners' capital accounts, £1,800

- salary of one partner, £10,000; the other partner does not receive a salary

- interest on partners' drawings, £700

If the remaining profits are shared equally, how much will each partner receive?

(a)	£10,500	
(b)	£11,400	
(c)	£12,300	
(d)	£16,400	

14.3   You have the following information about a partnership business:

- The financial year ends on 31 March.
- The partners are Amy, Bob and Caz.
- Interest on capital is allowed to the partners and is shown in the table below.
- Interest on drawings is charged to the partners and is shown in the table below.

	Amy	Bob	Caz
	£	£	£
Annual salaries	10,000	12,500	nil
Capital account balances, 31 March 20-5	60,000	35,000	26,000
Interest on capital for the year	3,250	1,750	1,400
Drawings for the year	30,000	28,500	8,500
Interest on drawings for the year	300	285	85

- The profit for distribution to the partners after appropriations is £43,000.
- Profits are shared in the following percentages: Amy 50%, Bob 30%, Caz 20%.

Prepare the current accounts for the partners for the year ended 31 March 20-6. Show clearly the balances carried down.

- You MUST enter zeros where appropriate.
- Do NOT use brackets, minus signs or dashes.

Select your entries from the following list:

Balance b/d, Balance c/d, Bank, Capital – Amy, Capital – Bob, Capital – Caz, Current – Amy, Current – Bob, Current – Caz, Drawings, Interest on capital, Interest on drawings, Salaries, Share of loss, Share of profit.

Current accounts

	Amy	Bob	Caz		Amy	Bob	Caz
	£	£	£		£	£	£
Balance b/d			210	Balance b/d	2,320	830	

14.4   You have the following information about a partnership business

> • The financial year ends on 31 March.
>
> • The partners are Uma, Val and Win.
>
> • Partners' annual salaries:
>   Uma   £10,400
>   Val   £15,200
>   Win   £16,750
>
> • Interest on partner's capital for the year:
>   Uma   £800
>   Val   £1,400
>   Win   £600
>
> • Interest charged on partners' drawings:
>   Uma   £240
>   Val   £360
>   Win   £290
>
> • The partners share the remaining profit of £18,000 as follows:
>   Uma   30%
>   Val   50%
>   Win   20%
>
> • Partners' drawings for the year:
>   Uma   £14,400
>   Val   £23,600
>   Win   £18,200

Prepare the current accounts for the partners for the year ended 31 March 20-4. Show clearly the balances carried down. You MUST enter zeros where appropriate. Do NOT use brackets, minus signs or dashes.

Current accounts

	Uma	Val	Win		Uma	Val	Win
	£	£	£		£	£	£
Balance b/d	0	0	300	Balance b/d	1,200	700	0

14.5 This Activity is about preparing a partnership statement of financial position.

You are preparing the statement of financial position for the RS Partnership as at 31 March 20-3. The partners are Ros and Sam.

All the necessary year-end adjustments have been made, except for the transfer of profit to the current accounts of the partners.

Before sharing profits, the balances of the partners' current accounts are:

- Ros £500 credit

- Sam £250 debit

Each partner is entitled to £5,500 profit share.

(a) Calculate the balance of each partner's current account after sharing profits. Indicate whether these balances are DEBIT or CREDIT.

Current account: Ros £	DEBIT / CREDIT
Current account: Sam £	DEBIT / CREDIT

Note: these balances will need to be transferred into the statement of financial position of the partnership which follows.

You have the following trial balance. All the necessary year-end adjustments have been made.

(b)   Prepare a statement of financial position for the partnership as at 31 March 20-3. You need to use the partners' current account balances that you have just calculated in (a). Do NOT use brackets, minus signs or dashes.

RS Partnership

Trial balance as at 31 March 20-3

	Dr £	Cr £
Accruals		230
Administration expenses	22,680	
Allowance for doubtful receivables		670
Allowance for doubtful receivables: adjustment		120
Bank	8,910	
Capital account – Ros		30,000
Capital account – Sam		25,000
Cash	490	
Closing inventory	11,670	11,670
Current account – Ros		500
Current account – Sam	250	
Depreciation charges	2,500	
Disposal of non-current asset		300
Office equipment at cost	32,000	
Office equipment: accumulated depreciation		7,900
Opening inventory	10,430	
Purchases	90,850	
Payables ledger control		13,370
Receivables ledger control	37,310	
Rent and rates	5,280	
Sales revenue		130,650
Value Added Tax		1,960
Total	222,370	222,370

RS Partnership

Statement of financial position as at 31 March 20-3

	Cost £	Accumulated depreciation £	Carrying amount £
Non-current assets			
Current assets			
Current liabilities			
Net current assets			
Net assets			
Financed by:	Ros	Sam	Total

14.6 You are preparing the partnership appropriation account for Amelia and Anya who run A&A Trading as a partnership.

The following information is available for the financial year ended 31 December 20-3:

- Profit for the year was £35,450.
- Profit is shared between Amelia and Anya in the ratio 70:30.
- Anya works in the business and receives a salary of £12,000; Amelia does not receive a salary.
- Partners' capitals are Amelia £50,000, Anya £20,000.
- Partners' drawings are Amelia £15,000, Anya £20,000.
- Interest on capitals is Amelia £1,000, Anya £400.
- Interest on drawings is Amelia £350, Anya £500.

(a) **You are to** complete the following appropriation account for the year ended 31 December 20-3.

All numbers should be shown to the nearest £ and as positives.

Select your descriptions from the following list: Amelia, Anya, Capital, Drawings, Interest charged on drawings, Interest on capital, Partners' salaries.

	Total £	Amelia £	Anya £
Profit/(loss) for the year			
Add			
Less appropriation of profits			
Profit available for distribution			
Profit share			
Amelia			
Anya			
Total profit distributed			

(b)   At the beginning of the financial year, 1 January 20-3, the balance on the partners' current accounts was Amelia £1,050 debit and Anya £850 credit.

You are to calculate the balance of the partners' current accounts at the end of the financial year, 31 December 20-3. Indicate whether the balances are debit or credit.

Current account: 31 December 20-3	£	Debit	Credit
Amelia			
Anya			

15 Using profitability ratios

Tutorial note: unless stated otherwise, calculate profitability ratios to two decimal places.

15.1 Gross profit margin is:

(a) Gross profit ÷ Revenue x 100/1	
(b) Cost of sales ÷ Revenue x 100/1	
(c) Gross profit ÷ Cost of sales x 100/1	
(d) Revenue ÷ Cost of sales x 100/1	

15.2 Net profit margin is:

(a) Profit for the year ÷ Capital employed x 100/1	
(b) Revenue ÷ Profit for the year x 100/1	
(c) Gross profit ÷ Revenue x 100/1	
(d) Profit for the year ÷ Revenue x 100/1	

15.3 From the following table, tick the items from the statement of profit or loss that are used in the calculation of gross profit margin and gross profit mark-up.

	Gross profit margin	Gross profit mark-up
Sales revenue		
Purchases		
Opening inventory		
Closing inventory		
Cost of sales		
Gross profit		
Expenses		
Net profit		
Capital employed		

15.4 The following information is taken from the statements of profit or loss of two businesses for the year ended 31 December 20-3:

	Cee	Dee
	£	£
Sales revenue	252,000	473,000
Cost of sales	181,000	327,000
GROSS PROFIT	71,000	146,000
Less Expenses	55,000	117,000
PROFIT FOR THE YEAR	16,000	29,000
Note: Capital employed	200,000	100,000

You are to calculate for each business:

- gross profit margin
- gross profit mark-up
- cost of sales/revenue percentage
- expenses/revenue percentage
- net profit margin
- return on capital employed

15.5 The following balances have been taken from the accounts of a business for the year ended 31 December 20-8:

	£
Purchases	88,000
Opening inventory	12,000
Sales revenue	165,000
Closing inventory	10,000

(a) State the formula for gross profit mark-up.

(b) Calculate the gross profit mark-up.

(c) State the formula for gross profit margin.

(d) Calculate the gross profit margin.

(e) State the formula for cost of sales in relation to revenue percentage.

(f) Calculate the cost of sales in relation to revenue percentage.

15.6 The following information is available for Daveco, a sole trader business, for the year ended 30 September 20-9:

	£
Sales revenue	220,000
Cost of sales	150,000
GROSS PROFIT	70,000
Less Expenses	48,000
PROFIT FOR THE YEAR	22,000
Note: Capital employed	150,000

You are to:

(a) Calculate profitability ratios for Daveco and put them into the table below.

	Daveco's ratios	Industry standard ratios
Gross profit margin		35.20%
Gross profit mark-up		54.32%
Cost of sales/revenue percentage		64.80%
Expenses/revenue percentage		25.20%
Net profit margin		10.00%
Return on capital employed		11.25%

(b) Comment on Daveco's ratios in comparison with the industry standard ratios shown in the table.

15.7 Johanna Fisher owns a sandwich and coffee shop situated on a trading estate where she has a good trade with people who work on the estate. Her friend has a similar shop on the high street of the town where they both live.

Johanna and her friend meet regularly and, from time to time, they talk business. They have decided to calculate and compare their profitability ratios and ask you to comment on them. The ratios are:

Profitability ratios	Johanna's ratios	Her friend's ratios
Gross profit margin	55.00%	50.00%
Gross profit mark-up	122.22%	100.00%
Cost of sales/revenue percentage	45.00%	50.00%
Shop wages/revenue percentage	35.00%	25.00%
Net profit margin	20.00%	25.00%
Return on capital employed	14.00%	18.00%

You are to provide comments on the above profitability ratios, indicating which is better or worse, and give guidance on how the ratios can aid planning, decision making and control for these businesses.

16 Incomplete records accounting

16.1 • Cost of sales for the year is £250,000.
  • Gross profit mark-up is 50%.

What are sales for the year (net of VAT)?

(a)	£375,000	
(b)	£125,000	
(c)	£250,000	
(d)	£500,000	

16.2 • Sales for the year are £240,000 (including VAT at 20%).
  • Gross profit margin is 30%.
  • Opening inventory is £15,000; closing inventory is £20,000.

What are purchases for the year (net of VAT)?

(a)	£260,000	
(b)	£160,000	
(c)	£140,000	
(d)	£145,000	

16.3 You are preparing accounts from incomplete records. Trade payables at the start of the year were £16,400. During the year, purchases on credit total £73,400, bank payments to trade payables total £68,100, purchases returns total £1,800, and discounts received total £400.

What is the trade payables figure at the end of the year?

(a)	£13,300	
(b)	£20,300	
(c)	£19,500	
(d)	£23,900	

16.4 Talib Zabbar owns a shop selling children's clothes. He is convinced that one of his employees is stealing goods from the shop. He asks you to calculate from the accounting records the value of inventory stolen. The following information is available for the year ended 31 March 20-2:

- sales for the year, £160,000
- opening inventory at the beginning of the year, £30,500
- purchases for the year, £89,500
- closing inventory at the end of the year, £21,500
- the gross profit margin achieved on all sales is 40%

You are to calculate the value of inventory stolen (if any) during the year ended 31 March 20-2.

Note: VAT is to be ignored on all transactions.

16.5 You are working on the accounts of a sole trader business. For the year ended 31 March 20-1 you have the following information:

• Trade payables at 1 April 20-0	£7,240
• Trade payables at 31 March 20-1	£6,180
• Bank payments to trade payables during the year	£51,420
• Cash purchases during the year	£1,730

(a) Calculate the purchases for the year ended 31 March 20-1.

£ [   ]

You are now working on the accounts of a different business. This business recently had a fire in its offices and the computer on which the accounting records are kept, together with the majority of the supporting paperwork and computer backups, were destroyed.

The business makes all its sales in cash.

You have been asked to produce some figures for the financial statements.

Each source of information below will help find some of the figures that are missing.

(b) For each source of information indicate the **one** missing figure that it will help to find. Put a tick in the relevant column of the table below.

Note: you do not have sufficient information to find all of the missing figures.

Source of information	Missing figures				
	Total sales	Cost of sales	Closing inventory	Profit for the year	Non-current assets
Bank statement					
Physical inventory count					
Gross profit margin					

16.6 This Activity is about finding missing figures in ledger accounts where the records are incomplete.

You are working on the financial statements of a business for the year ended 31 March 20-8. You have the following information:

Day book summaries for the year	Net £	VAT £	Total £
Sales	102,000	20,400	122,400
Purchases	64,000	12,800	76,800
Sales returns	1,800	360	2,160
Purchases returns	1,240	248	1,488

All sales and purchases are on credit terms.

Balances as at:	31 March 20-7 £	31 March 20-8 £
Trade receivables	16,250	18,108
Trade payables	10,380	not known

Further information:	Net £	VAT £	Total £
Administration expenses	22,000	4,400	26,400

Administration expenses are not included in the purchases figure in purchases day book.

Bank summary	Dr £		Cr £
Balance b/d	10,680	Travel expenses	5,290
Receivables ledger control	117,950	Administration expenses	26,400
Balance c/d	6,313	Payables ledger control	72,833
		HMRC for VAT	2,760
		Drawings	10,500
		Wages and salaries	17,160
	134,943		134,943

There were no discounts received on payments made to trade payables.

(a)   Find the missing discounts figure by preparing the receivables ledger control account for the year ended 31 March 20-8.

Receivables ledger control account

(b)   Find the closing balance on the payables ledger control account for the year ended 31 March 20-8.

Payables ledger control account

(c)   Find the closing balance on the VAT control account for the year ended 31 March 20-8.

Note: the business is not charged VAT on its travel expenses.

VAT control account

		Balance b/d	1,470

16.7 You are preparing the accounting records of Faye's business from incomplete information. The business is registered for VAT.

The following information relates to the financial year ended 31 December 20-4:

Day book summaries	Goods	VAT	Total
	£	£	£
Sales	120,350	24,070	144,420
Purchases	68,310	13,662	81,972

Balances	1 Jan 20-4	31 Dec 20-4
	£	£
Receivables ledger control	11,044	12,396
Payables ledger control	10,279	9,854

Bank summary			
Account name	**£**	**Account name**	**£**
Trade receivables	143,068	Balance b/d	3,964
Cash sales	15,240	HMRC VAT	12,065
		Payroll (no VAT)	40,132
		Trade payables	80,729
		Stationery	4,140
Balance c/d	2,722	Drawings	20,000
Total	161,030	Total	161,030

(a)   Using the information supplied, prepare the payables ledger control account for the year in order to find the missing purchases returns figure.

Select your account names from the following list: Balance b/d, Balance c/d, Bank, Purchases, Purchases returns, Sales, Sales returns.

Payables ledger control			
Account name	**£**	**Account name**	**£**
Total		Total	

(b)   Using the information supplied and your answer to (a) above, prepare the VAT control account for the year in order to show the balance c/d.

Select your account names from the following list: Balance b/d, Balance c/d, Bank, Cash sales, Purchases, Purchases returns, Sales, Sales returns, Stationery.

VAT control			
Account name	**£**	**Account name**	**£**
		Balance b/d	2,043
Total		Total	

Answers to chapter activities

1 The accounting system

1.1 **(a)** The **financial** accountant is mainly concerned with external reporting.

(b) The sales day book is an example of a book of **prime entry**.

(c) Receivables ledger contains the personal accounts of **trade receivables**.

(d) Sales account is contained in the **general** ledger.

(e) Income minus **expenses** equals **profit or loss**.

(f) **Assets** minus **liabilities** equals capital.

1.2 **(b)** Financial document; book of prime entry; double-entry bookkeeping; trial balance; financial statements (final accounts)

1.3 • asset of bank increases by £9,000
asset of cash increases by £1,000
capital increases by £10,000
assets £10,000 – liabilities £0 = capital £10,000

• asset of office equipment increases by £2,500
asset of bank decreases by £2,500
assets £10,000 – liabilities £0 = capital £10,000

• asset of bank increases by £2,000
liability of loan increases by £2,000
assets £12,000 – liabilities £2,000 = capital £10,000

• asset of machinery increases by £8,000
asset of bank decreases by £8,000
assets £12,000 – liabilities £2,000 = capital £10,000

• asset of office equipment increases by £2,000
liabilities of trade payables increases by £2,000
assets £14,000 – liabilities £4,000 = capital £10,000

1.4

	Assets	Liabilities	Capital
	£	£	£
(a)	10,000	0	10,000
(b)	20,000	7,500	12,500
(c)	16,750	6,250	10,500
(d)	17,030	4,350	12,680
(e)	17,290	5,425	11,865
(f)	24,003	6,709	17,294

1.5　**(a)**　Owner starts in business with capital of £8,000, comprising £7,000 in the bank and £1,000 in cash.

　　(b)　Purchases office equipment for £5,000, paid from the bank.

　　(c)　Receives a loan of £5,000, paid into the bank.

　　(d)　Purchases office equipment for £500, paid in cash.

　　(e)　Purchases machinery for £6,000, paid from the bank.

　　(f)　Owner introduces £2,000 additional capital, paid into the bank.

2 Double-entry bookkeeping

2.1 **(a)** A **debit** entry records an account which gains value, or records an asset, or an expense.

(b) In the books of a business, the **credit** side of bank account records money paid out.

(c) In capital account, the initial capital contributed by the owner of the business is recorded on the **credit** side.

(d) Office equipment is an example of a **non-current** asset.

(e) The purchase of a printer for use in the office is classed as **capital** expenditure.

(f) Repairs to a printer are classed as **revenue** expenditure.

2.2 **ANDREW KING**

(a)

Dr			Bank account			Cr
20-4			£	20-4		£
1 Oct	Capital		7,500	4 Oct	Machinery	4,000
12 Oct	T Richards: loan		1,500	6 Oct	Office equipment	2,250
18 Oct	Commission received		200	11 Oct	Rent paid	400
				15 Oct	Wages	500
				20 Oct	Drawings	250
				25 Oct	Wages	450

(b)

Dr		Capital account			Cr
20-4		£	20-4		£
			1 Oct	Bank	7,500

Dr		Machinery account		Cr
20-4		£	20-4	£
4 Oct	Bank	4,000		

Dr		Office equipment account		Cr
20-4		£	20-4	£
6 Oct	Bank	2,250		

Dr		Rent account		Cr
20-4		£	20-4	£
11 Oct	Bank	400		

Dr		Tina Richards: loan account			Cr
20-4		£	20-4		£
			12 Oct	Bank	1,500

Dr		Wages account		Cr
20-4		£	20-4	£
15 Oct	Bank	500		
25 Oct	Bank	450		

Dr		Commission received account			Cr
20-4		£	20-4		£
			18 Oct	Bank	200

Dr		Drawings account		Cr
20-4		£	20-4	£
20 Oct	Bank	250		

2.3 (c)

Debit	**Credit**
Purchases account	Trade payables account

2.4 (c)

Debit	**Credit**
Trade payables account	Purchases returns account

2.5

Transaction	Account debited	Account credited
(a)	purchases	bank
(b)	bank	sales
(c)	purchases	Teme Traders
(d)	L Harris	sales
(e)	Teme Traders	purchases returns (returns out)
(f)	sales returns (returns in)	L Harris
(g)	bank	D Perkins: loan
(h)	cash	bank

2.6 **PERSHORE PACKAGING**

Dr		Purchases account			Cr
20-8		£	20-8		£
4 Jan	AB Supplies Limited	250			
20 Jan	Bank	225			

Dr		AB Supplies Limited			Cr
20-8		£	20-8		£
15 Jan	Bank	250	4 Jan	Purchases	250

Dr		Sales account			Cr
20-8		£	20-8		£
			5 Jan	Bank	195
			7 Jan	Cash	150
			18 Jan	L Lewis	145

Dr		Bank account			Cr
20-8		£	20-8		£
5 Jan	Sales	195	15 Jan	AB Supplies Limited	250
11 Jan	J Johnson: loan	1,000	20 Jan	Purchases	225
28 Jan	L Lewis	145	29 Jan	Mercia Office Supplies Ltd	160

Dr		Cash account			Cr
20-8		£	20-8		£
7 Jan	Sales	150	22 Jan	Wages	125

Dr		J Johnson: loan account			Cr
20-8		£	20-8		£
			11 Jan	Bank	1,000

Dr		L Lewis			Cr
20-8		£	20-8		£
18 Jan	Sales	145	28 Jan	Bank	145

Dr		Wages account			Cr
20-8		£	20-8		£
22 Jan	Cash	125			

Dr		Office equipment account			Cr
20-8		£	20-8		£
26 Jan	Mercia Office Supplies Ltd	160			

Dr		Mercia Office Supplies Limited			Cr
20-8		£	20-8		£
29 Jan	Bank	160	26 Jan	Office equipment	160

2.7   SONYA SMITH

Dr		Purchases account		Cr
20-6		£	20-6	£
2 Feb	G Lewis	200		
17 Feb	G Lewis	160		

Dr		Sales account		Cr
20-6		£	20-6	£
			4 Feb L Jarvis	150
			8 Feb G Patel	240

Dr		G Lewis			Cr
20-6		£	20-6		£
10 Feb	Bank	190	2 Feb	Purchases	200
10 Feb	Discounts received	10	17 Feb	Purchases	160
24 Feb	Bank	152			
24 Feb	Discounts received	8			
		360			360

Dr		L Jarvis			Cr
20-6		£	20-6		£
4 Feb	Sales	150	12 Feb	Bank	147
			12 Feb	Discounts allowed	3
		150			150

Dr		G Patel			Cr
20-6		£	20-6		£
8 Feb	Sales	240	19 Feb	Bank	234
			19 Feb	Discounts allowed	6
		240			240

Dr		Bank account			Cr
20-6		£	20-6		£
12 Feb	L Jarvis	147	10 Feb	G Lewis	190
19 Feb	G Patel	234	24 Feb	G Lewis	152

Dr		Discounts received account			Cr
20-6		£	20-6		£
			10 Feb	G Lewis	10
			24 Feb	G Lewis	8

Dr		Discounts allowed account		Cr
20-6		£	20-6	£
12 Feb	L Jarvis	3		
19 Feb	G Patel	6		

3 Balancing accounts and the trial balance

3.1 (d) Purchases

3.2 (b) Capital

3.3

TINA WONG
Trial balance as at 30 November 20-9

	Dr £	Cr £
Bank		1,855
Capital		9,000
Cash	85	
Office equipment	2,500	
Purchases	2,419	
Purchases returns		102
Sales		4,164
Sales returns	354	
Trade payables		1,082
Trade receivables	2,115	
Vehicle	7,500	
Wages	1,230	
	16,203	16,203

3.4 **(a)**

LORNA FOX
Trial balance as at 31 March 20-1

	Dr £	Cr £
Administration expenses	10,240	
Bank overdraft		1,050
Capital		155,440
Cash	150	
Drawings	9,450	
Interest paid	2,350	
Loan from bank		20,000
Machinery	40,000	
Premises	125,000	
Purchases	96,250	
Sales		146,390
Sales returns	8,500	
Telephone	3,020	
Trade payables		10,545
Trade receivables	10,390	
Travel expenses	1,045	
Value Added Tax		1,950
Wages	28,980	
	335,375	335,375

(b) See *Financial Accounting: Preparing Financial Statements Tutorial*, Chapter 3 and page 45. The explanation should be appropriate for someone who does not understand accounting.

3.5 **(a)** "You made an error of **principle** when you debited the cost of fuel for the van to Vans Account."

(b) "There is a 'bad figure' on a purchases invoice – we have read it as £35 when it should be £55. It has gone through our accounts wrongly so we have an error of **original entry** to put right."

(c) "Who was in charge of that trainee last week? He has entered the payment for the electricity bill on the debit side of the bank and on the credit side of electricity – a **reversal** of **entries**."

(d) "I found this purchase invoice from last week in amongst the copy statements. As we haven't put it through the accounts we have an error of **omission**."

(e) "I've had the bookkeeper from D Jones Limited on the phone concerning the statements of account that we sent out the other day. She says that there is a sales invoice charged that she knows nothing about. I wonder if we have made an error of **commission** and it should be for T Jones' account?"

3.6 (a) and (c)

MARK TANSALL

Dr			Bank account				Cr
20-4			£	20-4			£
1 Jan	Capital		10,000	4 Jan	Rent paid		500
11 Jan	Sales		2,400	5 Jan	Shop fittings		5,000
12 Jan	Sales		2,000	25 Jan	Purchases		3,000
20 Jan	Sales		1,500	27 Jan	Sales returns		280
22 Jan	Sales		2,250	31 Jan	Balance c/d		9,370
			18,150				18,150
1 Feb	Balance b/d		9,370	4 Feb	Rent paid		500
2 Feb	Sales		2,720	5 Feb	Shop fittings		1,550
10 Feb	Sales		3,995	12 Feb	Tech Software		7,500
22 Feb	Sales		1,930	19 Feb	Datasoft Ltd		5,000
24 Feb	Sales		2,145	28 Feb	Balance c/d		9,760
26 Feb	Sales		4,150				
			24,310				24,310
1 Mar	Balance b/d		9,760				

Dr		Capital account				Cr
20-4		£	20-4			£
			1 Jan	Bank		10,000

Dr		Rent paid account				Cr
20-4		£	20-4			£
4 Jan	Bank	500	28 Feb	Balance c/d		1,000
4 Feb	Bank	500				
		1,000				1,000
1 Mar	Balance b/d	1,000				

Dr		Shop fittings account				Cr
20-4		£	20-4			£
5 Jan	Bank	5,000	28 Feb	Balance c/d		6,550
5 Feb	Bank	1,550				
		6,550				6,550
1 Mar	Balance b/d	6,550				

Dr		Purchases account			Cr
20-4		£	20-4		£
7 Jan	Tech Software	7,500	31 Jan	Balance c/d	15,500
16 Jan	Datasoft Ltd	5,000			
25 Jan	Bank	3,000			
		15,500			15,500
1 Feb	Balance b/d	15,500	28 Feb	Balance c/d	22,130
15 Feb	Tech Software	4,510			
25 Feb	Associated Software	2,120			
		22,130			22,130
1 Mar	Balance b/d	22,130			

Dr		Tech Software			Cr
20-4		£	20-4		£
12 Feb	Bank	7,500	7 Jan	Purchases	7,500
28 Feb	Balance c/d	4,510	15 Feb	Purchases	4,510
		12,010			12,010
			1 Mar	Balance b/d	4,510

Dr		Sales account			Cr
20-4		£	20-4		£
31 Jan	Balance c/d	10,645	11 Jan	Bank	2,400
			12 Jan	Bank	2,000
			20 Jan	Bank	1,500
			22 Jan	Bank	2,250
			29 Jan	Teme College	2,495
		10,645			10,645
28 Feb	Balance c/d	25,585	1 Feb	Balance b/d	10,645
			2 Feb	Bank	2,720
			10 Feb	Bank	3,995
			22 Feb	Bank	1,930
			24 Feb	Bank	2,145
			26 Feb	Bank	4,150
		25,585			25,585
			1 Mar	Balance b/d	25,585

Dr	Datasoft Limited		Cr
20-4	£	20-4	£
19 Feb Bank	5,000	16 Jan Purchases	5,000

Dr	Sales returns account		Cr
20-4	£	20-4	£
27 Jan Bank	280	28 Feb Balance c/d	425
23 Feb Teme College	145		
	425		425
1 Mar Balance b/d	425		

Dr	Teme College		Cr
20-4	£	20-4	£
29 Jan Sales	2,495	23 Feb Sales returns	145
		28 Feb Balance c/d	2,350
	2,495		2,495
1 Mar Balance b/d	2,350		

Dr	Associated Software		Cr
20-4	£	20-4	£
		25 Feb Purchases	2,120

(b)   **Trial balance as at 31 January 20-4**

	Dr	Cr
	£	£
Bank	9,370	
Capital		10,000
Rent paid	500	
Shop fittings	5,000	
Purchases	15,500	
Tech Software		7,500
Sales		10,645
Datasoft Limited		5,000
Sales returns	280	
Teme College	2,495	
	33,145	33,145

(d)   **Trial balance as at 28 February 20-4**

	Dr £	Cr £
Bank	9,760	
Capital		10,000
Rent paid	1,000	
Shop fittings	6,550	
Purchases	22,130	
Tech Software		4,510
Sales		25,585
Sales returns	425	
Teme College	2,350	
Associated Software		2,120
	42,215	42,215

4   Financial statements – the extended trial balance

4.1   (d)   Cash

4.2   (b)   Sales revenue

4.3 EXTENDED TRIAL BALANCE

MATT SMITH

31 DECEMBER 20-3

Account name	Ledger balances		Adjustments		Statement of profit or loss		Statement of financial position	
	Dr £	Cr £	Dr £	Cr £	Dr £	Cr £	Dr £	Cr £
Opening inventory	14,350				14,350			
Purchases	114,472				114,472			
Sales revenue		259,688				259,688		
Business rates	13,718				13,718			
Heating and lighting	12,540				12,540			
Wages and salaries	42,614				42,614			
Vehicle expenses	5,817				5,817			
Advertising	6,341				6,341			
Premises at cost	75,000						75,000	
Office equipment at cost	33,000						33,000	
Vehicles at cost	21,500						21,500	
Receivables ledger control	23,854						23,854	
Bank	1,235						1,235	
Cash	125						125	
Capital		62,500						62,500
Drawings	12,358						12,358	
Loan from bank		35,000						35,000
Payables ledger control		14,258						14,258
Value Added Tax		5,478						5,478
Closing inventory: statement of profit or loss		16,280				16,280		
Closing inventory: statement of financial position	16,280						16,280	
Profit/loss for the year					66,116			66,116
	393,204	393,204			275,968	275,968	183,352	183,352

4.4 EXTENDED TRIAL BALANCE

CLARE LEWIS

31 DECEMBER 20-4

Account name	Ledger balances		Adjustments		Statement of profit or loss		Statement of financial position	
	Dr £	Cr £	Dr £	Cr £	Dr £	Cr £	Dr £	Cr £
Receivables ledger control	18,600						18,600	
Payables ledger control		11,480						11,480
Value Added Tax		1,870						1,870
Bank		4,610						4,610
Capital		25,250						25,250
Sales revenue		144,810				144,810		
Purchases	96,318				96,318			
Opening inventory	16,010				16,010			
Salaries	18,465				18,465			
Heating and lighting	1,820				1,820			
Rent and rates	5,647				5,647			
Vehicles at cost	9,820						9,820	
Office equipment at cost	5,500						5,500	
Sundry expenses	845				845			
Vehicle expenses	1,684				1,684			
Drawings	13,311						13,311	
Closing inventory: statement of profit or loss		13,735				13,735		
Closing inventory: statement of financial position	13,735						13,735	
Profit/loss for the year					17,756			17,756
	201,755	201,755			158,545	158,545	60,966	60,966

5 Accruals and prepayments

5.1   (a)   A liability and an expense accrued

5.2   (d)   Income accrued

5.3 **(a)** **Selling expenses**

	£		£
Bank	12,700	Accrued expenses (reversal)	400
		Statement of profit or loss	11,750
		Prepaid expenses	550
	12,700		12,700

(b) **Vehicle expenses**

		£			£
20-1 1 Apr	Prepaid expenses (reversal)	150	20-2 31 Mar	Statement of profit or loss	7,630
20-2 31 Mar	Bank	7,200			
20-2 31 Mar	Accrued expenses	280			
		7,630			7,630

(c)

Account	£	Dr £	Cr £
Accrued expenses			280
Capital	45,000		45,000
Discounts allowed	470	470	
Drawings	12,500	12,500	
Interest paid	380	380	
Office equipment at cost	24,500	24,500	
Prepaid expenses		550	
Purchases returns	2,740		2,740

5.4 EXTENDED TRIAL BALANCE

CINDY HAYWARD

30 JUNE 20-4

Account name	Ledger balances Dr £	Ledger balances Cr £	Adjustments Dr £	Adjustments Cr £	Statement of profit or loss Dr £	Statement of profit or loss Cr £	Statement of financial position Dr £	Statement of financial position Cr £
Capital		90,932						90,932
Drawings	10,000		200				10,200	
Purchases	148,500			200	148,300			
Sales revenue		210,900				210,900		
Repairs to buildings	848				848			
Vehicles at cost	15,000						15,000	
Vehicle expenses	1,540		85		1,625			
Land and buildings at cost	185,000						185,000	
Loan from bank		110,000						110,000
Bank	540						540	
Shop fittings at cost	12,560						12,560	
Wages	30,280		560		30,840			
Discounts allowed	135				135			
Discounts received		1,319				1,319		
Rates and insurance	2,690			255	2,435			
Receivables ledger control	3,175						3,175	
Payables ledger control		8,295						8,295
Heating and lighting	3,164				3,164			
General expenses	4,680				4,680			
Sales returns	855				855			
Purchases returns		1,221				1,221		
Opening inventory	6,210				6,210			
Value Added Tax		2,510						2,510
Closing inventory: statement of profit or loss				7,515		7,515		
Closing inventory: statement of financial position			7,515				7,515	
Accruals				645				645
Prepayments			255				255	
Profit/loss for the year					21,863			21,863
	432,692	432,692	1,100	1,100	220,955	220,955	234,245	234,245

6 Depreciation of non-current assets

6.1 (b) £6,860

6.2 (c) 30%

6.3 (c) Loss on disposal of £30

6.4 (b)

Debit	**Credit**
Disposals account	Statement of profit or loss

6.5 (a)

Year 1	£1,600
Year 2	£1,280
Total	£2,880

(b) **Machine at cost**

Balance b/d	£8,000	Disposals	£8,000
	£8,000		£8,000

Machine: disposals

Machine at cost	£8,000	Machine: accumulated depreciation	£2,880
		Bank	£4,800
		Statement of profit or loss	£320
	£8,000		£8,000

Bank

Machine disposals	£4,800	Balance c/d	£5,760
Value Added Tax	£960		
	£5,760		£5,760

(c)

gain	
loss	✔

6.6 EXTENDED TRIAL BALANCE

WINTERGREEN SUPPLIES

31 DECEMBER 20-6

Account name	Ledger balances		Adjustments		Statement of profit or loss		Statement of financial position	
	Dr £	Cr £	Dr £	Cr £	Dr £	Cr £	Dr £	Cr £
Premises at cost	120,000						120,000	
Premises: accumulated depreciation		7,200		2,400				9,600
Bank loan		52,800						52,800
Capital		70,000						70,000
Receivables ledger control	11,900						11,900	
Payables ledger control		11,500						11,500
Drawings	6,750						6,750	
Cash	150						150	
Opening inventory	4,200				4,200			
Office equipment at cost	5,000						5,000	
Office equipment: accumulated depreciation		1,000		1,000				2,000
Vehicles at cost	10,000						10,000	
Vehicles: accumulated depreciation		2,000		2,000				4,000
Bank		750						750
Sales revenue		194,850				194,850		
Purchases	154,000				154,000			
Wages	20,500			560	19,940			
Sundry expenses	9,500		500		10,000			
Value Added Tax		1,750						1,750
Disposal of non-current asset		150				150		
Closing inventory: statement of profit or loss		5,200				5,200		
Closing inventory: statement of financial position	5,200						5,200	
Accruals				500				500
Prepayments			560				560	
Depreciation charges			5,400		5,400			
Profit/loss for the year					6,660			6,660
	347,200	347,200	6,460	6,460	200,200	200,200	159,560	159,560

7 Irrecoverable debts and allowance for doubtful receivables

7.1 (c)

Debit	**Credit**
Irrecoverable debts account	T Neal's account

Tutorial note: where control accounts – see Chapter 10 of the *Tutorial* – are in use, the credit entry will be to receivables ledger control account.

7.2 (a) Decrease profit for the year

7.3 (b) £2,270

7.4

Year	Statement of profit or loss			Statement of financial position	
	Dr Irrecoverable debts £	Dr Allowance for doubtful receivables: adjustment £	Cr Allowance for doubtful receivables: adjustment £	Dr Receivables ledger control £	Cr Allowance for doubtful receivables £
20-5	1,800	2,585	–	103,400	2,585
20-6	2,400	245	–	113,200	2,830
20-7	1,400	–	110	108,800	2,720

7.5 **(a)** **Irrecoverable debts**

	£		£
Receivables ledger control (Craven Traders)	75	Statement of profit or loss	240
Receivables ledger control (Harris and Co)	110		
Receivables ledger control (P Mahon)	55		
	240		240

(b) **Allowance for doubtful receivables**

		£			£
20-6 31 Dec	Allowance for doubtful receivables: adjustment	50	20-6 01 Jan	Balance b/d	300
20-6 31 Dec	Balance c/d	250			
		300			300

(c)

Account	Ledger balances		Adjustments	
	Dr £	Cr £	Dr £	Cr £
Allowance for doubtful receivables		300	50	
Allowance for doubtful receivables: adjustment				50
Irrecoverable debts			240	
Payables ledger control		8,960		
Receivables ledger control	12,740			240
Vehicles at cost	20,000			
Vehicles: accumulated depreciation		11,200		
Wages	22,850			

7.6 EXTENDED TRIAL BALANCE

JANE JONES

31 DECEMBER 20-5

Account name	Ledger balances Dr £	Ledger balances Cr £	Adjustments Dr £	Adjustments Cr £	Statement of profit or loss Dr £	Statement of profit or loss Cr £	Statement of financial position Dr £	Statement of financial position Cr £
Receivables ledger control	37,200			2,200			35,000	
Payables ledger control		30,640						30,640
Value Added Tax		4,280						4,280
Bank	14,640						14,640	
Capital		50,500						50,500
Sales revenue		289,620				289,620		
Purchases	182,636				182,636			
Opening inventory	32,020				32,020			
Wages and salaries	36,930				36,930			
Heat and light	3,640				3,640			
Rent and rates	11,294			2,190	9,104			
Vehicles at cost	20,000						20,000	
Vehicles: accumulated depreciation		4,000		3,200				7,200
Machinery at cost	10,000						10,000	
Machinery: accumulated depreciation		1,000		900				1,900
Sundry expenses	1,690		270		1,960			
Vehicle expenses	3,368				3,368			
Drawings	26,622						26,622	
Closing inventory: statement of profit or loss		34,000				34,000		
Closing inventory: statement of financial position	34,000						34,000	
Accruals				270				270
Prepayments			2,190				2,190	
Depreciation charges			4,100		4,100			
Irrecoverable debts			2,200		2,200			
Allowance for doubtful receivables				1,750				1,750
Allowance for doubtful receivables: adjustment			1,750		1,750			
Profit/loss for the year					45,912			45,912
	414,040	414,040	10,510	10,510	323,620	323,620	142,452	142,452

8 Framework of accounting

8.1

User	Use of information
HM Revenue & Customs	• To assess if the business is able to pay VAT and tax due
Bank	• To see how much profit has been made • To check that the business will be able to make interest payments and repayments • To assess how much of the business is being funded by the lender • To see what security is available to cover loans
Potential investor	• To see how much profit has been made • To see how much can be paid out in drawings or dividends • To see the asset value of the business and whether it has increased or decreased • To assess if the business will continue in the future

8.2

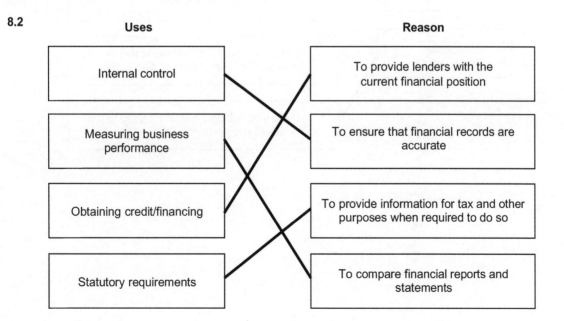

Uses	Reason
Internal control	To provide lenders with the current financial position
Measuring business performance	To ensure that financial records are accurate
Obtaining credit/financing	To provide information for tax and other purposes when required to do so
Statutory requirements	To compare financial reports and statements

8.3

Accounting principle	Explanation
Business entity	The financial statements record and report on the activities of one particular business
Going concern	The presumption is that the business to which the financial statements relate will continue to trade in the foreseeable future
Prudence	Caution is exercised when making judgements under conditions of uncertainty; where there is any doubt, a conservative figure for profit and the valuation of assets should be reported

8.4 (a) Accruals

8.5

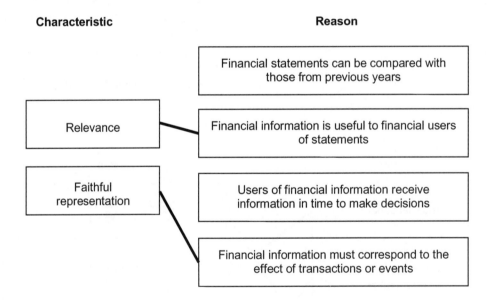

Characteristic

Reason

Financial statements can be compared with those from previous years

Relevance

Financial information is useful to financial users of statements

Faithful representation

Users of financial information receive information in time to make decisions

Financial information must correspond to the effect of transactions or events

8.6 (d) Understandability

8.7 **(a)** The use of the word 'material' means that the amount of the misstatement must be significant in relation to the size of the business so as to affect the decisions of users.

(b) **(1)** If profit is **overstated** investors may be encouraged to buy a stake in the business.

(2) If profit is **understated** HM Revenue & Customs will receive a lower amount of tax than should be paid.

(3) If sales turnover is **understated** HM Revenue & Customs will receive a lower amount of VAT than should be paid.

(4) If assets are **overvalued** a lender may find that security for a loan is less than expected.

8.8

Principle   **Application**

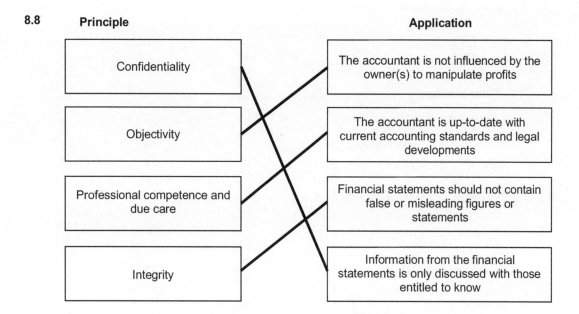

8.9 Professional scepticism is an attitude of:

• having a questioning mind

• being alert to conditions which may indicate possible misstatement due to error or fraud

• making a critical assessment of evidence

8.10 **(a)** IAS 2 *Inventories* states that inventories are to be valued at **the lower of cost and net realisable value**.

(b)

FIFO	
£54	
£61	✔
£60	
£48	
£40	
£135	

Tutorial notes:

The closing inventory is:

	units bought (20 + 10 + 10)	=	40
less	units sold (8 + 16)	=	24
equals	closing inventory	=	16

FIFO

6 units at £3.50	=	£21.00
10 units at £4.00	=	£40.00
16 units	=	£61.00

8.11 **(a)**   Sales revenue for the half year: £

·   product Y, 220 units at £10.00 each   =   2,200.00
·   product Z, 340 units at £16.00 each   =   5,440.00

·   total sales   =   7,640.00

(b)   Product Y: £

    20 units at £4.20 per unit   =   84.00
100 units at £3.80 per unit   =   380.00
  80 units at £4.50 per unit   =   360.00

200 units   =   824.00

Product Z: £

    60 units at £10.50 per unit   =   630.00
140 units at £10.00 per unit   =   1,400.00

200 units   =   2,030.00

(c)   £

·   Product Y   =   824.00   (cost price)
·   Product Z   =   1,950.00   (net realisable value)

                                                        =   2,774.00

(d)   Purchases   £

·   product Y   =   1,728.00
·   product Z   =   5,400.00

                                                                 7,128.00

Less closing inventory   =   2,774.00

Cost of sales   4,354.00

8.12 £144,000, ie £240,000 x (100 – 40)/100

8.13 £240,000, ie £288,000 x 100/(100 + 20)

8.14

Journal

Date	Details	Reference	Dr	Cr
			£	£
20-6				
31 Dec	Inventory	GL	25,000	
	Statement of profit or loss	GL		25,000
	Transfer of closing inventory as at 31 December 20-6 to the statement of profit or loss			

9 Accounting for capital transactions

9.1 (b) Goodwill

9.2 (d) Quarterly electricity bill

9.3 (c) Cost of materials used to extend the premises

9.4 (b) Debited to the statement of profit or loss

9.5

		Capital expenditure	Revenue expenditure
(a)	Purchase of vehicles	✔	
(b)	Depreciation of vehicles		✔
(c)	Rent paid on premises		✔
(d)	Wages and salaries		✔
(e)	Legal fees relating to the purchase of property	✔	
(f)	Redecoration of office		✔
(g)	Installation of air-conditioning in office	✔	
(h)	Wages of own employees used to build extension to the office	✔	
(i)	Installation and setting up of a new machine	✔	

9.6   **Depreciation calculations:**

	20-2	20-3	20-4	Total
	£	£	£	£
Van 1	4,000	3,000	–	7,000
Van 2	4,000	3,000	2,250	9,250
Van 3	–	–	4,500	4,500
Van 4	–	–	4,500	4,500
Total	8,000	6,000	11,250	25,250

Dr			Vehicles at cost account			Cr
20-2			£	20-2		£
01 Jan	Bank		16,000	31 Dec	Balance c/d	32,000
01 Jan	Bank		16,000			
			32,000			32,000
20-3				20-3		
01 Jan	Balance b/d		32,000	31 Dec	Balance c/d	32,000
20-4				20-4		
01 Jan	Balance b/d		32,000	20 Mar	Disposals	16,000
01 Jan	Bank		18,000	31 Dec	Balance c/d	52,000
01 Jan	Bank		18,000			
			68,000			68,000
20-5				20-5		
01 Jan	Balance b/d		52,000			

Dr	Depreciation charges account		Cr
20-2	£	20-2	£
31 Dec Vehicles: accumulated depreciation	8,000	31 Dec Statement of profit or loss	8,000
20-3		20-3	
31 Dec Vehicles: accumulated depreciation	6,000	31 Dec Statement of profit or loss	6,000
20-4		20-4	
31 Dec Vehicles: accumulated depreciation	11,250	31 Dec Statement of profit or loss	11,250

Dr		Vehicles: accumulated depreciation account			Cr
20-2		£	20-2		£
31 Dec	Balance c/d	8,000	31 Dec	Depreciation charges	8,000
20-3			20-3		
31 Dec	Balance c/d	14,000	01 Jan	Balance b/d	8,000
			31 Dec	Depreciation charges	6,000
		14,000			14,000
20-4			20-4		
20 Mar	Disposals	7,000	01 Jan	Balance b/d	14,000
31 Dec	Balance c/d	18,250	31 Dec	Depreciation charges	11,250
		25,250			25,250
20-5			20-5		
			01 Jan	Balance b/d	18,250

Dr		Vehicle disposals account			Cr
20-4		£	20-4		£
20 Mar	Vehicles	16,000	20 Mar	Vehicles: accumulated depreciation	7,000
			20 Mar	Bank	8,000
			20 Mar	Statement of profit or loss (loss on disposal)	1,000
		16,000			16,000

9.7

EXTRACT FROM NON-CURRENT ASSET REGISTER							
Description/serial no	Acquisition date	Cost £	Depreciation charges £	Carrying amount £	Funding method	Disposal proceeds £	Disposal date
Machinery							
Moulding machine	12/08/-3	10,000.00			Cash		
Year end 31/03/-4			2,000.00	8,000.00			
Year end 31/03/-5			2,000.00	6,000.00			
Year end 31/03/-6			2,000.00	4,000.00			
Pressing machine	17/06/-5	2,660.00			Cash		
Year end 31/03/-6			532.00	2,128.00			
Vehicles							
AB69 TPJ	11/06/-3	16,400.00			Cash		
Year end 31/03/-4			4,100.00	12,300.00			
Year end 31/03/-5			3,075.00	9,225.00			
Year end 31/03/-6			0.00	0.00		8,000.00	14/02/-6
AB75 PZE	01/01/-5	15,200.00			Part-exchange		
Year end 31/03/-5			3,800.00	11,400.00			
Year end 31/03/-6			2,850.00	8,550.00			

Tutorial notes:

- installation of the pressing machine is capitalised

- the service contract is revenue expenditure

9.8

Item	Understated	Overstated	No effect
Net profit			✔
Current assets		✔	
Current liabilities			✔
Non-current assets	✔		

10 Control accounts

10.1

Error		Difference	No difference
(a)	Sales returns day book was undercast by £100	✔	
(b)	A credit note for £75 was credited to the account of Martley Traders instead of Martley Manufacturing – both are receivables ledger accounts		✔
(c)	The receivables ledger account of C Fernandez, £125, has been written off as irrecoverable, but no entry has been made in receivables ledger control account	✔	
(d)	A set-off entry for £45 has been incorrectly recorded as £54 in the receivables ledger control account and in the receivables ledger account		✔

10.2

		£
Total of list of payables ledger balances		55,946
Adjustment for (a)	add	18
Adjustment for (b)	subtract	200
Adjustment for (c)	subtract	141
Adjustment for (d)	subtract	225
Revised total to agree with payables ledger control account		55,398

10.3

Dr				VAT Control Account			Cr
20-1			£	20-1			£
31 Jan	Purchases		11,046	1 Jan	Balance b/d		6,240
31 Jan	Sales returns		722	31 Jan	Purchases returns		498
31 Jan	Non-current assets		1,845	31 Jan	Discounts received		164
31 Jan	Bank		6,240	31 Jan	Credit sales		19,047
31 Jan	Balance c/d		6,096				
			25,949				25,949
				1 Feb	Balance b/d		6,096

10.4

Dr	Wages and Salaries Control Account		Cr

20-2		£	20-2		£
28 Feb	Bank	11,367	28 Feb	Wages expenses	17,342
28 Feb	Pension fund	2,025			
28 Feb	Trade union fees	295			
28 Feb	HM Revenue & Customs	3,655			
		17,342			17,342

10.5

Adjustment number	Debit £	Credit £
1		120
3		100
4		95

10.6

Adjustment number	Debit £	Credit £
1		500
2	190	
4	280	

10.7

Adjustment number	Debit £	Credit £
2		360
3		90
4		120

10.8 **(a)** £530.66 debit

(b)

Bank reconciliation statement as at 30 April 20-2	£
Closing bank statement balance	546.24
Less unpresented cheques	
Stanton Ltd	276.33
Add outstanding lodgements	
Groves & Co	260.75
Closing cash book balance	530.66

11 The journal and correction of errors

11.1 (d)   Bank payment to a trade payable

11.2 (c)

Debit		**Credit**	
Stationery	£25	Office equipment	£25

11.3 (a)

Debit		**Credit**	
Suspense	£36	Vehicle repairs	£36
Vehicle repairs	£63	Suspense	£63

11.4

		Profit increases	Profit decreases
(a)	Sales account overcast		✔
(b)	Closing inventory undervalued	✔	
(c)	Telephone expenses account undercast		✔
(d)	Discounts received omitted	✔	
(e)	Depreciation charges for vehicles omitted		✔
(f)	Irrecoverable debt not written off		✔
(g)	Decrease in allowance for doubtful receivables not made	✔	

11.5 **(a)** **Journal**

	Dr £	Cr £
Irrecoverable debts	300	
Receivables ledger control		300

(b) **Journal**

	Dr £	Cr £
Office equipment	4,000	
Suspense		4,000

(c) **Journal**

	Dr £	Cr £
Inventory	*18,140	
Statement of profit or loss		*18,140

* lower of cost and net realisable value: £18,380 – £240

(d) **Journal**

	Dr £	Cr £
VAT	920	
Suspense		920
VAT	920	
Suspense		920

11.6 Extended trial balance

Ledger account	Ledger balances		Adjustments		Statement of profit or loss		Statement of financial position	
	Dr £	Cr £	Dr £	Cr £	Dr £	Cr £	Dr £	Cr £
Allowance for doubtful receivables		1,200	100					1,100
Allowance for doubtful receivables adjustment				100		100		
Bank	15,300						15,300	
Capital		30,000						30,000
Closing inventory			25,230	25,230		25,230	25,230	
Depreciation charges			2,500		2,500			
Office equipment at cost	20,000						20,000	
Office equipment: accumulated depreciation		8,500		2,500				11,000
Office expenses	12,700		500		13,200			
Opening inventory	22,680				22,680			
Payroll expenses	25,920			350	25,570			
Purchases	85,500		400		85,900			
Payables ledger control		25,270						25,270
Rent and rates	5,400			250	5,150			
Sales		151,200				151,200		
Receivables ledger control	30,380						30,380	
Suspense	300		600	900				
VAT		2,010						2,010
Profit/loss for the year					21,530			21,530
	218,180	218,180	29,330	29,330	176,530	176,530	90,910	90,910

Tutorial note: the debit balance on suspense account is cleared by the debit adjustment of £600 (£350 and £250), and the credit adjustment of £900 (£500 and £400).

11.7

Journal number: 278	31 December 20-5	
Account name	**Debit**	**Credit**
	£	£
Inventory	9,180	
Closing inventory: spl		9,180
Bank	5,000	
Capital		5,000
Discounts received	90	
Suspense		90
Stationery	115	
Suspense		115

12 Preparing financial statements

12.1 (a) Opening inventory + purchases – closing inventory

12.2 (d) Statement of profit or loss

12.3 (c) The excess of current assets over current liabilities

12.4 Business A: gross profit £8,000, profit for year £4,000

Business B: gross profit £17,000, expenses £7,000

Business C: sales £36,500, profit for year £6,750

Business D: purchases £25,500, expenses £9,800

Business E: opening inventory £8,350, loss for year £1,700

Business F: closing inventory £4,600, expenses £15,000

12.5 **(a)** Assets: £49,220

Liabilities: £21,890

Capital: £27,330

(b) An intangible non-current asset which does not have material substance

12.6 **(a)** £53,220

(b)

	Debit	Credit	No change
Non-current assets	✔		
Trade receivables			✔
Trade payables			✔
Bank		✔	
Capital			✔

(c) (a) A bank loan repayable in two years' time

12.7

> **LUCY CHAZAL**
> **STATEMENT OF PROFIT OR LOSS**
> **for the year ended 31 December 20-4**
>
> | | £ | £ |
> |---|---:|---:|
> | Sales revenue | | 397,242 |
> | Opening inventory | 32,147 | |
> | Purchases | 201,318 | |
> | Closing inventory | −35,419 | |
> | | | |
> | Cost of sales | | 198,046 |
> | | | |
> | **Gross profit** | | 199,196 |
> | Less expenses: | | |
> | Business rates | 18,210 | |
> | Heating and lighting | 23,680 | |
> | Payroll expenses | 77,211 | |
> | Vehicle expenses | 7,619 | |
> | Advertising | 15,483 | |
> | | | |
> | | | 142,203 |
> | | | |
> | **Profit for the year** | | 56,993 |

STATEMENT OF FINANCIAL POSITION as at 31 December 20-4

	£	£	£
Non-current assets			
Premises at cost			150,000
Office equipment at cost			25,000
Vehicles at cost			32,500
			207,500
Current assets			
Inventory (closing)		35,419	
Trade receivables		33,482	
Bank		2,704	
Cash		525	
Total current assets		72,130	
Current liabilities			
Trade payables	35,138		
Value Added Tax	6,211		
Total current liabilities		41,349	
Net current assets			30,781
			238,281
Non-current liabilities			
Loan from bank			60,000
Net assets			178,281
Financed by:			
Capital			
Opening capital			148,500
Add Profit for the year			56,993
			205,493
Less Drawings			27,212
Closing capital			178,281

12.8

LISA JAMES
STATEMENT OF PROFIT OR LOSS
for the year ended 31 March 20-7

	£	£
Sales revenue		127,500
Sales returns		–2,150
Net sales revenue		125,350
Opening inventory	17,540	
Net purchases*	74,840	
	92,380	
Closing inventory	–19,960	
Cost of sales		72,420
Gross profit		52,930
Add income: Discounts received		230
		53,160
Less expenses:		
Discounts allowed	470	
Carriage out	1,540	
Other expenses	35,830	
		37,840
Profit for the year		15,320

*Net purchases:	£
purchases	77,200
– purchases returns	3,040
+ carriage in	680
= net purchases	74,840

12.9

Transaction	Increase	Decrease	No effect
New non-current assets paid for from the business bank account			✔
Owner's computer transferred into the business	✔		
Loss for the year		✔	
Owner's drawings		✔	
Owner arranges a bank overdraft for the business			✔

12.10

Statement	True	False
The owner's drawings account has a debit balance	✔	
Net current assets is current assets plus current liabilities		✔
Trade payables is a current asset		✔
A bank overdraft is a current liability	✔	
Profit for the year is gross profit plus expenses		✔
Cost of sales is opening inventory plus purchases minus closing inventory	✔	

13 Sole trader financial statements

13.1 (a) £14,730

13.2

Item	Income	Expense
Gain on disposal of non-current asset	✔	
Decrease in allowance for doubtful receivables	✔	
Irrecoverable debts		✔
Discounts allowed		✔
Depreciation charges		✔
Commission received	✔	

13.3 (d) £17,740

13.4 **(a)**

Tysoe Trading Statement of profit or loss for the year ended 31 March 20-6		
	£	£
Sales revenue		140,680
Opening inventory	11,450	
Purchases	64,330	
Closing inventory	−10,200	
Cost of sales		65,580
Gross profit		75,100
Less expenses:		
Depreciation charges	2,500	
Discounts allowed	490	
General expenses	25,720	
Payroll expenses	29,610	
Rent and rates	7,240	
Total expenses		65,560
Profit/loss for the year		9,540

(b) (c) As a current liability

(c) (a) The business has made a gain on disposal

13.5

	RHIANNA AITKEN		
	STATEMENT OF PROFIT OR LOSS		
	for the year ended 31 March 20-1		
		£	£
Sales revenue			166,240
Opening inventory		18,890	
Purchases		85,330	
Closing inventory		−22,450	
Cost of sales			81,770
Gross profit			84,470
Add other income:			
Disposal of non-current asset			600
			85,070
Less expenses:			
Allowance for doubtful receivables: adjustment		220	
Shop wages		35,560	
Heat and light		2,680	
Rent and rates		10,570	
Depreciation charges		4,750	
Irrecoverable debts		150	
			53,930
Profit for the year			31,140

STATEMENT OF FINANCIAL POSITION
as at 31 March 20-1

Non-current assets	£ Cost	£ Accumulated depreciation	£ Carrying amount
Shop fittings	36,000	12,380	23,620
Current assets			
Inventory		22,450	
Trade receivables		*3,230	
Prepayments		440	
Total current assets		26,120	
Current liabilities			
Trade payables	11,490		
Value Added Tax	1,720		
Accruals	590		
Bank	2,360		
Total current liabilities		16,160	
Net current assets			9,960
Net assets			33,580
Financed by:			
Capital			
Opening capital			27,500
Add Profit for the year			31,140
			58,640
Less Drawings			25,060
Closing capital			33,580

* receivables ledger control £4,110 *minus* allowance for doubtful receivables £880

13.6

Capital			
Account name	**£**	**Account name**	**£**
Drawings	10,330	Balance b/d	55,200
Drawings	1,270	Statement of profit or loss	18,750
Balance c/d	68,350	Bank	5,000
		Computer	1,000
Total	79,950	Total	79,950

14 Partnership financial statements

14.1 (c)   Partnership agreement

14.2 (a)   £10,500

14.3   Current accounts

	Amy	Bob	Caz		Amy	Bob	Caz
	£	£	£		£	£	£
Balance b/d			210	Balance b/d	2,320	830	
Drawings	30,000	28,500	8,500	Salaries	10,000	12,500	0
Interest on drawings	300	285	85	Interest on capital	3,250	1,750	1,400
Balance c/d	6,770		1,205	Share of profit	21,500	12,900	8,600
				Balance c/d		805	
	37,070	28,785	10,000		37,070	28,785	10,000

14.4   Current accounts

	Uma	Val	Win		Uma	Val	Win
	£	£	£		£	£	£
Balance b/d	0	0	300	Balance b/d	1,200	700	0
Drawings	14,400	23,600	18,200	Salaries	10,400	15,200	16,750
Interest on drawings	240	360	290	Interest on capital	800	1,400	600
Balance c/d	3,160	2,340	2,160	Profit share	5,400	9,000	3,600
	17,800	26,300	20,950		17,800	26,300	20,950

14.5 (a)   Current account: Ros £6,000   CREDIT

Current account: Sam £5,250   CREDIT

(b)   **RS Partnership**

Statement of financial position as at 31 March 20-3

	Cost	Accumulated depreciation	Carrying amount
Non-current assets	£	£	£
Office equipment	32,000	7,900	24,100
Current assets			
Inventory		11,670	
Trade receivables		*36,640	
Bank		8,910	
Cash		490	
Total current assets		57,710	
Current liabilities			
Trade payables	13,370		
Value Added Tax	1,960		
Accruals	230		
Total current liabilities		15,560	
Net current assets			42,150
Net assets			66,250
Financed by:	**Ros**	**Sam**	**Total**
Capital accounts	30,000	25,000	55,000
Current accounts	6,000	5,250	11,250
	36,000	30,250	66,250

*receivables ledger control £37,310 *minus* allowance for doubtful receivables £670

Note: bank £8,910 + cash £490 = cash and cash equivalents £9,400.

14.6 (a)

	Total	Amelia	Anya
	£	£	£
Profit/(loss) for the year	35,450		
Add			
Interest charged on drawings	850	350	500
Less appropriation of profits			
Interest on capital	1,400	1,000	400
Partners' salaries	12,000	-	12,000
Profit available for distribution	22,900		
Profit share			
Amelia	16,030		
Anya	6,870		
Total profit distributed	22,900		

(b)

Current account: 31 December 20-3	£	Debit	Credit
Amelia	630		✔
Anya	380	✔	

Workings:

Amelia (£1,050) – £350 + £1,000 + £16,030 – £15,000

Anya £850 – £500 + £400 + £12,000 + £6,870 – £20,000

15 Using profitability ratios

15.1 (a) Gross profit ÷ Revenue x 100/1

15.2 (d) Profit for the year ÷ Revenue x 100/1

15.3

	Gross profit margin	Gross profit mark-up
Sales revenue	✔	
Purchases		
Opening inventory		
Closing inventory		
Cost of sales		✔
Gross profit	✔	✔
Expenses		
Net profit		
Capital employed		

15.4 CEE

- gross profit margin = £71,000 ÷ £252,000 x 100/1 = 28.17%
- gross profit mark-up = £71,000 ÷ £181,000 x 100/1 = 39.23%
- cost of sales/revenue percentage = £181,000 ÷ £252,000 x 100/1 = 71.83%
- expenses/revenue percentage = £55,000 ÷ £252,000 x 100/1 = 21.83%
- net profit margin = £16,000 ÷ £252,000 x 100/1 = 6.35%
- return on capital employed = £16,000 ÷ £200,000 x 100/1 = 8.00%

DEE

- gross profit margin = £146,000 ÷ £473,000 x 100/1 = 30.87%
- gross profit mark-up = £146,000 ÷ £327,000 x 100/1 = 44.65%
- cost of sales/revenue percentage = £327,000 ÷ £473,000 x 100/1 = 69.13%

- expenses/revenue percentage = £117,000 ÷ £473,000 x 100/1 = 24.74%
- net profit margin = £29,000 ÷ £473,000 x 100/1 = 6.13%
- return on capital employed = £29,000 ÷ £100,000 x 100/1 = 29.00%

15.5 **(a)** gross profit ÷ cost of sales x 100/1

(b) £75,000 ÷ £90,000 x 100/1 = 83.33%

(c) gross profit ÷ revenue x 100/1

(d) £75,000 ÷ £165,000 x 100/1 = 45.45%

(e) cost of sales ÷ revenue x 100/1

(f) £90,000 ÷ £165,000 x 100/1 = 54.55%

15.6 **(a)**

	Daveco's ratios	Industry standard ratios
Gross profit margin	31.82%	35.20%
Gross profit mark-up	46.67%	54.32%
Cost of sales/revenue percentage	68.18%	64.80%
Expenses/revenue percentage	21.82%	25.20%
Net profit margin	10.00%	10.00%
Return on capital employed	14.67%	11.25%

(b)
- Daveco has a lower gross profit margin than the industry standard. This is confirmed by a lower gross profit mark-up and higher cost of sales/revenue percentage. This indicates that Daveco is less efficient at buying in goods for resale and/or has lower selling prices than the industry standard.

- Daveco's expenses/revenue % is lower than the industry standard, which is a sign of a more efficient business.

- Net profit margin is identical for Daveco and the industry standard. This shows that any weakness of Daveco in buying and selling prices has been counteracted with the lower expenses/revenue %.

- Return on capital employed is above the industry standard, which shows that Daveco is giving a good return to the owner.

- The conclusion is that, while Daveco should seek to improve its buying and selling prices, it is better than the industry average in other aspects, particularly return on capital employed.

15.7 • These businesses are both sandwich and coffee shops, but located in different areas – Johanna's on a trading estate and her friend's on the high street. As such, despite selling similar products, they will have a different range of customers.

• Johanna's business has a higher gross profit margin than that of her friend. This is confirmed by her higher gross profit mark-up and lower cost of sales/revenue percentage. This indicates that Johanna is buying in goods for resale at lower prices and/or has higher selling prices than her friend.

• For shop wages, the ratio against revenue shows that Johanna has the higher percentage. Such a difference might be caused if Johanna employs full-time staff, but her friend is able to employ part-time staff as and when required. As a consequence of higher labour costs, Johanna's net profit margin is lower than that of her friend.

• Return on capital employed appears to be reasonable for both businesses, bearing in mind the risks of running a business. Johanna has a lower ROCE.

• In conclusion, both businesses are performing well, but they can learn from each other – Johanna to look at reducing her wages costs, and her friend to review her buying and selling prices.

16 Incomplete records accounting

16.1 (a) £375,000

Workings: £250,000 + £125,000 profit

16.2 (d) £145,000

Workings: sales £200,000 net of VAT x 70% = cost of sales £140,000 + closing inventory £20,000 = £160,000 – opening inventory £15,000

16.3 (c) £19,500

Workings: £16,400 + £73,400 – £68,100 – £1,800 – £400

16.4

TALIB ZABBAR		
CALCULATION OF INVENTORY LOSS FOR THE YEAR ENDED 31 MARCH 20-2		
	£	£
Opening inventory		30,500
Purchases		89,500
Cost of inventory available for sale		120,000
Sales	160,000	
Normal gross profit margin (40%)	–64,000	
Cost of sales		96,000
Estimated closing inventory		24,000
Actual closing inventory		–21,500
Value of inventory loss		2,500

16.5 **(a)** £52,090

Workings: £51,420 – £7,240 + £6,180 + £1,730

(b)

Source of information	Missing figures				
	Total sales	Cost of sales	Closing inventory	Profit for year	Non-current assets
Bank statement	✔				
Physical inventory count			✔		
Gross sales margin		✔			

16.6 **(a)** **Receivables ledger control account**

Balance b/d	16,250	Sales returns	2,160
Sales	122,400	Bank	117,950
		Discounts allowed	432
		Balance c/d	18,108
	138,650		138,650

(b) **Payables ledger control account**

Purchases returns	1,488	Balance b/d	10,380
Bank	72,833	Purchases	76,800
Balance c/d	12,859		
	87,180		87,180

(c)   **VAT control account**

Purchases	12,800	Balance b/d	1,470
Sales returns	360	Sales	20,400
Administration expenses	4,400	Purchases returns	248
Bank	2,760		
Discounts allowed	72		
Balance c/d	1,726		
	22,118		22,118

16.7   **(a)**

Payables ledger control			
Account name	**£**	**Account name**	**£**
Bank	80,729	Balance b/d	10,279
Purchases returns	1,668	Purchases	81,972
Balance c/d	9,854		
Total	92,251	Total	92,251

(b)

VAT control			
Account name	**£**	**Account name**	**£**
Purchases	13,662	Balance b/d	2,043
Stationery	690	Sales	24,070
Bank	12,065	Cash sales	2,540
Balance c/d	2,514	Purchases returns	278
Total	28,931	Total	28,931

Practice
assessment 1

Assessment information

- This practice assessment contains **6 tasks** and you should attempt to complete **every** task.

- Each task is independent. You will not need to refer to your answers from previous tasks.

- Read every task carefully to make sure you understand what is required.

- Where the date is relevant, it is given in the task data.

- Both minus signs and brackets can be used to indicate negative numbers **unless** task instructions state otherwise.

- You must use a full stop to indicate a decimal point. For example, write 100.57, **not** 100,57 or 10057.

- You may use a comma to indicate a number in the thousands, but you don't have to. For example, 10000 and 10,000 are both acceptable.

Task 1

This task is about using day books and accounting for and monitoring non-current assets.

(a) (i) Complete the following statements about books of prime entry.

Statement	Option
A list of credit sales made, compiled from invoices issued, is recorded initially in the …	
Discounts from suppliers for prompt payment of invoices are recorded initially in the …	

Choose your options from the following list: Cash book, Discounts allowed day book, Discounts received day book, Journal, Purchases day book, Purchases returns day book, Sales day book, Sales returns day book.

(ii) An item of capital expenditure has been wrongly classified as revenue expenditure. What is the effect on the following items in the financial statements?

Item	Understated ✔	Overstated ✔	No effect ✔
Net profit			
Current assets			
Current liabilities			
Non-current assets			

(b) Which **two** of the following accounting principles relate BEST to depreciation?

Accounting principle	✔
Prudence	
Business entity	
Going concern	
Materiality	
Accruals	

(c) You are working for Sam Smythe, a sole trader with a financial year-end date of 31 March 20-0.

- Sam is registered for VAT.
- Sam has bought a new machine. VAT can be reclaimed on this machine.
- The cost excluding VAT was £6,000; this was paid from the bank.
- The residual value is expected to be £2,000 excluding VAT.
- Sam's depreciation policy for machines is to use the straight-line basis over five years. A full year's depreciation is applied in the year of acquisition.
- Depreciation has already been entered into the accounts for the existing machines.

(i) Calculate the depreciation charges for the year on the new machine.

£ [   ] machinery depreciation charge

Make entries to account for:

- the acquisition of the new machine
- the depreciation charge on the new machine

On each account, show clearly the balance carried down or transferred to the statement of profit or loss, as appropriate, and the total for each.

Select your entries from the following list:

Balance b/d, Balance c/d, Bank, Disposals, Machinery accumulated depreciation, Machinery at cost, Machinery depreciation charges, Payables ledger control, Purchases, Purchases ledger control, Receivables ledger control, Sales, Statement of profit or loss.

Machinery at cost   £   £

Balance b/d	25,000		
Total		**Total**	

Machinery depreciation charges £ £

	£		£
Balance b/d	5,000		
Total		Total	

Machinery accumulated depreciation £ £

	£		£
		Balance b/d	10,000
Total		Total	

(ii) Sam's business keeps a non-current asset register of the machinery owned by the business. Which **one** of the following statements regarding a non-current asset register is true?

It shows the carrying amount of each machine	
It proves legal ownership of each machine	
It shows how much each machine will be sold for when it is disposed	
It shows when it is time to replace each machine	

(iii) Sam's business has sold a car which originally cost £10,000. The proceeds of £4,000 have been paid into the bank. **Note:** no VAT was charged to the person who bought the car.

Which of the following entries for the proceeds is correct?

Debit Disposals; Credit Bank	
Debit Vehicle at cost; Credit Bank	
Debit Bank; Credit Disposals	
Debit Bank; Credit Vehicles at cost	

Task 2

This task is about recording period end adjustments.

Imogen is in business making wooden garden furniture. You are preparing her accounts for the year ended 30 June 20-2.

(a) **(i)** Identify whether each of the following items of expenditure should or should not be included in the valuation of Imogen's inventory at cost.

Item	Included in valuation ✔	Not included in valuation ✔
Purchase cost of wood		
Labour costs to make the furniture		
Selling costs to market the furniture		
Costs of storage of finished furniture		

(ii) Imogen has not made an adjustment for a prepayment of wages.

Identify how her assets and profits are affected by this omission.

Item	No effect ✔	Understated ✔	Overstated ✔
Assets			
Profit			

(b) You are looking at rent paid by Imogen for the year ended 30 June 20-2:

- On 30 June 20-1 an entry of £500 was made in the rent paid account in relation to a prepayment. This entry needs to be reversed from the prepaid expenses account into the current year.

- The cash book for the year shows payments for rent of £7,500. This includes a payment of £2,100 for the three months ending 31 August 20-2.

Complete the rent paid account for the year ended 30 June 20-2 showing the amount transferred to the statement of profit or loss. Dates are not required.

Select your account entries from the following list: Accrued expenses, Accrued expenses reversal, Balance b/d, Balance c/d, Cash book, Prepaid expenses, Prepaid expenses reversal, Statement of profit or loss.

Rent paid account			
	£		£
Total		Total	

(c) Imogen asks you to write off an irrecoverable debt and to make accounting adjustments to her allowance for doubtful receivables:

- The balance of receivables ledger control account at 30 June 20-2 is £25,425.

- Imogen wishes to write off as irrecoverable the account of Elmhurst Garden Centre which has a balance of £225. Ignore VAT.

- Imogen has a policy of adjusting the allowance for doubtful receivables to 2.5% of receivables. The allowance for doubtful receivables at 1 July 20-1 was £655.

Prepare the journal entries relating to the irrecoverable debt and to the allowance for doubtful receivables at 30 June 20-2.

Journal number: 564	30 June 20-2	
Account name	Debit £	Credit £

Select your account names from: Allowance for doubtful receivables, Allowance for doubtful receivables adjustment, Elmhurst Garden Centre, Irrecoverable debts, Receivables ledger control, Sales revenue, Statement of profit or loss.

Task 3

This task is about producing, adjusting, checking and extending the trial balance.

(a)   (i)   Complete the following statements about the classification of accounts.

Statement	Option
Irrecoverable debts are …	
A bank overdraft is …	

Choose your options from the following list: a non-current asset, a current asset, a non-current liability, a current liability, a part of capital (equity), an income item, an expense item.

(ii)   A trial balance will disclose certain errors.

Identify whether each of the errors listed below will be disclosed or will not be disclosed by a trial balance. Ignore VAT.

Error	Error disclosed by the trial balance ✔	Error not disclosed by the trial balance ✔
A bank payment for telephone expenses has been recorded on the debit side of both the cash book and telephone expenses account.		
A sales invoice has been omitted from all accounting records.		
The balance of purchases returns account has been calculated incorrectly.		
A bank payment of £85 for stationery has been recorded as £58 in both accounts.		

(b)   Lana has received her bank statement for the month of June 20-2 and has asked you to complete the bank reconciliation statement. At 30 June 20-2:

- Her bank statement shows an overdrawn balance of £230.56 debit.

- Her cash book shows a credit balance of £120.83.

The following items are outstanding on either the bank statement or the cash book:

- Bank charges of £63.50 are on the bank statement but not in the cash book.

- A Faster Payment for £318.97 received from Wyvern Ltd, a customer, is on the bank statement but not in the cash book.

- A cheque for £473.44 from Gomez & Co, which was paid into the bank yesterday, has been entered in the cash book but is not shown on the bank statement.

- A payment for £108.24 by cheque from Lana to Kelly Ltd has been entered in the cash book but is not shown on the bank statement.

(i) What is the amended cash book balance at 30 June 20-2 after dealing with the items? Indicate whether it is debit or credit.

£		debit	credit

(ii) Complete Lana's bank reconciliation statement as at 30 June 20-2. Show any overdrafts as negative figures; all other figures should be positive.

Select your entries from the following list: Bank charges, Gomez & Co, Kelly Ltd, Wyvern Ltd.

Bank reconciliation statement as at 30 June 20-2	£
Closing bank statement balance	
Less	
Add	
Closing cash book balance	

(c) The trial balance for Isabella's business has been produced for the year ended 30 June 20-3. The debit column totals £102,685 and the credit column totals £101,745.

Prepare the entries to correct the following errors using the journal layout below. Dates and narratives are not required.

- The closing inventory has not been recorded in the accounts. It is valued at £6,290.

- A bank transfer for rent paid of £750 (no VAT) has been recorded in the correct accounts but on the incorrect side of each account.

- The balance of office expenses account, £1,560, has been calculated wrongly and should be £1,650.

- A new computer for the office costing £1,020 (including VAT) has been correctly recorded in the bank and VAT accounts but has not been recorded in office equipment account.

Tutorial note: where appropriate, use a single journal entry (one debit, one credit) rather than two entries.

Select your account names from the following list: Bank, Capital, Closing inventory: sfp*, Closing inventory: spl**, Inventory, Office equipment, Office expenses, Rent paid, Rent received, Suspense.

*   statement of financial position

**   statement of profit or loss

Journal number: 176	30 June 20-3	
Account name	**Debit** £	**Credit** £

(d)   The extended trial balance (on the next page) for the year is part completed. **You are to** finish extending the trial balance, including calculation of the profit or loss – specify in the appropriate space in the first column whether it is a profit or a loss for the year.

Account name	Ledger balances		Adjustments		Statement of profit or loss		Statement of financial position	
	Dr £	Cr £	Dr £	Cr £	Dr £	Cr £	Dr £	Cr £
Accrual of wages				230				230
Bank	9,420						9,420	
Capital		35,000		10,500				45,500
Closing inventory			9,450	9,450				
Depreciation charges	4,700							
Drawings			10,500				10,500	
Expenses	26,081			346	25,735			
Machinery at cost	23,500						23,500	
Machinery accumulated depreciation		7,920						7,920
Opening inventory	8,190							
Payables ledger control		7,368						7,368
Prepayment of expenses			346				346	
Purchases	58,484				58,484			
Receivables ledger control	13,378						13,378	
Rent receivable		2,765				2,765		
Sales		117,784				117,784		
Wages	27,084		230		27,314			
*								
TOTAL	170,837	170,837	20,526	20,526				

* Select your entry from Profit for the year, Loss for the year.

Task 4

This task is about producing financial statements for sole traders and partnerships.

(a) **(i)** Identify whether each of the following transactions would lead to an increase, a decrease, or no change in the owner's capital.

Transaction	Increase ✔	Decrease ✔	No change ✔
Owner arranges a bank overdraft			
Loss for the year			
Owner takes goods for personal use			
Owner transfers her computer into the business			

(ii) Identify whether the following statements about partnership statements of financial position are true or false.

Statement	True ✔	False ✔
The statement of financial position shows the year-end balances on each partner's capital and current account.		
A debit balance on a partner's current account means that the partner has drawn out more than his/her share of the profit.		

(b) The following information is required to answer tasks (b) (i) and (b) (ii).

Sara and Toni run Sarton Supplies as a partnership. Their trial balance at 31 March 20-1 is shown below.

Sarton Supplies
Trial balance as at 31 March 20-1

	Dr £	Cr £
Accruals		400
Administration expenses	16,210	
Bank	15,330	
Capital account – Sara as at 1 April 20-0		25,000
Capital account – Toni as at 1 April 20-0		22,500
Cash	180	
Closing inventory	6,090	6,090
Current account – Sara		2,620
Current account – Toni	460	
Depreciation charges	4,750	
Discounts received		160
Drawings – Sara	15,460	
Drawings – Toni	7,380	
Irrecoverable debts	120	
Machinery at cost	29,770	
Machinery accumulated depreciation		12,800
Opening inventory	5,150	
Other expenses	9,120	
Purchases	45,930	
Payables ledger control		5,108
Receivables ledger control	15,360	
Sales		95,320
VAT		1,312
TOTAL	171,310	171,310

Additional information:

- Profits and losses are shared between Sara and Toni in the ratio 60:40.
- Toni works in the business and is entitled to a salary of £12,000. Sara is not entitled to a salary.
- Interest on capital, Sara £750, Toni £675.
- Interest on drawings, Sara £225, Toni £105.

(i) Complete the statement of profit or loss for Sarton Supplies for the year ended 31 March 20-1.

All numbers should be shown to the nearest £.

Profit figures should be shown as positive and loss figures should be shown as negative. All other figures should be shown as positive.

Select your entries from the following list:

Administration expenses, Capital account – Sara, Capital account – Toni, Cash, Closing inventory, Current account – Sara, Current account – Toni, Depreciation charges, Discounts received, Irrecoverable debts, Machinery accumulated depreciation, Opening inventory, Other expenses, Purchases.

Sarton Supplies		
Statement of profit or loss for the year ended 31 March 20-1		
	£	£
Sales revenue		95,320
Less:		
Cost of sales		
Gross profit		
Add:		
Less:		
Total expenses		
Profit/Loss for the year		

(ii) Complete the following appropriation account for Sarton Supplies for the year ended 31 March 20-1.

All numbers should be shown to the nearest £.

Profit figures should be shown as positive and loss figures should be shown as negative. All other figures should be shown as positive.

Select your entries from the following list:

Capital, Drawings, Interest on drawings, Interest on capital, Partners' salaries.

Appropriation account for the year ended 31 March 20-1	Total £	Sara £	Toni £
Profit/(loss) for the year			
Add			
Less appropriation of profits			
Profit available for distribution			
Profit share			
Sara			
Toni			
Total profit distributed			

Task 5

This task is about accounting principles, qualities of useful financial information, and interpreting financial statements using profitability ratios.

(a) **(i)** Identify the accounting principle being described in each of the following.

Description	Accounting principle
Inventory is valued at the lower of cost and net realisable value.	
Income and expenses are matched to relate to the same goods and services and the same accounting period.	
Depreciation of non-current assets is made at 10% a year, using the straight-line method.	
Financial statements are prepared on the basis that the business will continue to trade in the foreseeable future.	

Select your accounting principles from the following list: Accruals, Business entity, Consistency, Going concern, Materiality, Prudence.

(ii) Identify the qualitative characteristics described below.

Description	Characteristic
Financial information is useful to the users of financial statements.	
Users of financial statements receive information quickly enough to enable decisions to be made.	

Select your characteristics from the following list: Comparability, Faithful representation, Relevance, Timeliness, Understandability, Verifiability.

(b) Identify whether each of the statements about profitability ratios is true or false.

Statement	True ✔	False ✔
Profitability ratios measure profit against the denominators of inventory, trade receivables or trade payables.		
Businesses use profitability ratios to aid control, decision-making and planning of the business.		
Profitability ratios can highlight symptoms within a business, but the cause will need to be investigated.		
The gross profit margin for a food supermarket and a furniture retailer should be very similar.		

(c) You have the following information about a business.

Statement of profit or loss extract	£
Sales revenue	530,300
Gross profit	120,260
Expenses	65,280
Profit/loss for the year	54,980
Statement of financial position extract	**£**
Non-current assets	250,590
Current assets	65,240
Current liabilities	30,320
Non-current liabilities	120,500
Capital	165,010

(i) Calculate the following ratios (to TWO decimal places) from the information above.

Gross profit margin (%)	
Return on capital employed (%)	

(ii) A business has calculated that its expense/revenue percentage is lower this year than last year.

Identify whether the following statements about the decrease in the ratio are true or false.

Statement	True ✔	False ✔
The decrease could have been caused by sales revenue rising during the year.		
The decrease could have been caused by reduced revenue expenditure during the year.		

Task 6

This task is about preparing accounting records from incomplete information.

(a) A trader has annual credit sales to credit customers of £110,380 including VAT, and has a policy of allowing credit customers to settle their accounts three weeks after the sale is made.

Identify which **one** of the following is most likely to be the balance of receivables ledger control account at the end of the financial year?

£6,400	
£9,200	
£110,380	

(b) You have the following information about a business for its year ended 31 March 20-5.

- It is not registered for VAT.

- The trader operates with a gross profit margin of 40%.

- Inventory at 1 April 20-4 was £10,500.

- Sales of £77,300 were made.

- Purchases were recorded as £47,930.

Using this information, complete the following tasks:

(i) Calculate the cost of sales for the year ended 31 March 20-5.

£ _____

(ii) Calculate the value of closing inventory at 31 March 20-5.

£ _____

(iii) You compare this closing inventory figure with the results of the physical inventory count at the year-end. The total physical inventory value is £500 higher than your calculation.

Which **one** of the following could explain this?

	✔
A high value item has not been included in the closing inventory figure	
The trader has made drawings of goods during the year	
Some inventory items have been taken for use in the office	
Some sales returns items have been missed in the physical count	

(iv) Update the value of closing inventory to account for the difference above.

£ _____

(c) You are preparing the accounting records of Tammy's business from incomplete information. The business is registered for VAT.

The following information relates to the financial year ended 31 March 20-1:

Day book summaries	Goods Net £	VAT £	Total £
Sales	134,000	26,800	160,800
Purchases	82,000	16,400	98,400

Balances	1 Apr 20-0 £	31 Mar 20-1 £
Receivables ledger control	18,275	23,465
Payables ledger control	10,384	12,658

Bank summary			
Account name	**£**	**Account name**	**£**
Balance b/d	10,770	HMRC VAT	7,245
Trade receivables	152,490	Payroll (no VAT)	51,390
Cash sales	10,320	Trade payables	102,845
		Drawings	17,500
Balance c/d	5,400		
Total	178,980	Total	178,980

(i) Using the information supplied, prepare the receivables ledger control account for the year in order to find the missing sales returns figure.

Select your account names from the following list: Balance b/d, Balance c/d, Bank, Purchases, Purchases returns, Sales, Sales returns.

Receivables ledger control			
Account name	**£**	**Account name**	**£**
Total		Total	

(ii) Using the information supplied and your answer to (i) above, prepare the VAT control account for the year in order to show the balance c/d.

Select your account names from the following list: Balance b/d, Balance c/d, Bank, Cash sales, Purchases, Sales, Sales returns.

VAT control			
Account name	**£**	**Account name**	**£**
		Balance b/d	2,140
Total		Total	

Practice
assessment 2

Assessment information

- This practice assessment contains **6 tasks** and you should attempt to complete **every** task.

- Each task is independent. You will not need to refer to your answers from previous tasks.

- Read every task carefully to make sure you understand what is required.

- Where the date is relevant, it is given in the task data.

- Both minus signs and brackets can be used to indicate negative numbers **unless** task instructions state otherwise.

- You must use a full stop to indicate a decimal point. For example, write 100.57, **not** 100,57 or 10057.

- You may use a comma to indicate a number in the thousands, but you don't have to. For example, 10000 and 10,000 are both acceptable.

Task 1

This task is about using day books and accounting for and monitoring non-current assets.

(a) **(i)** Complete the following statements about books of prime entry.

Statement	Option
Credit notes received for goods sent back to suppliers are recorded initially in the …	
The book of prime entry for cash purchases is the …	

Choose your options from the following list: Cash book, Discounts allowed day book, Discounts received day book, Journal, Purchases day book, Purchases returns day book, Sales day book, Sales returns day book.

(ii) Classify the following items of expenditure to either capital expenditure or revenue expenditure.

Items of expenditure	Capital expenditure ✔	Revenue expenditure ✔
Cost of a new vehicle		
Cost of insurance for vehicles		
Cost of an extension to the premises		
Cost of delivery for a new machine		

(iii) Complete the following statements about depreciation by selecting from the options below.

Depreciation charge for the year is recorded in the …	
The carrying amount of a non-current asset is recorded in the …	

Choose your options from the following list: Bank statement, Cash book, Payables ledger control account, Purchases day book, Receivables ledger control account, Sales day book, Statement of financial position, Statement of profit or loss.

(b) You are working for Lizzie Groves, a sole trader with a financial year-end date of 30 June 20-1.
- Lizzie is registered for VAT.
- Lizzie has bought a new computer for use in the office. VAT can be reclaimed on this computer.
- The cost including VAT was £2,700; this was paid from the bank.
- The residual value is expected to be £500 excluding VAT.
- Lizzie's depreciation policy for computers is to use the straight-line basis over five years. A full year's depreciation is applied in the year of acquisition.
- Depreciation has already been entered into the accounts for the other office computers.

(i) Calculate the depreciation charges for the year on the new computer.

£ _____ depreciation charge

Make entries to account for:
- the acquisition of the new computer
- the depreciation charge on the new computer

On each account, show clearly the balance carried down or transferred to the statement of profit or loss, as appropriate, and the total for each.

Select your entries from the following list:
Balance b/d, Balance c/d, Bank, Computers accumulated depreciation, Computers at cost, Computers depreciation charges, Disposals, Payables ledger control, Statement of profit or loss, Purchases, Receivables ledger control, Sales.

Computers at cost

	£		£
Balance b/d	9,500		
Total		**Total**	

Computers depreciation charges £ £

Balance b/d	2,000		
Total		Total	

Computers accumulated depreciation £ £

		Balance b/d	4,000
Total		Total	

(ii) Lizzie's business has purchased a new machine trading in an old machine as part exchange.

The cost of the old machine was £4,000 net of VAT, and accumulated depreciation at the date of part exchange is £2,400.

The cost of the new machine is £6,000 + VAT and Lizzie receives a part exchange allowance of £1,000 + VAT for the old machine. She pays the balance from the bank.

Complete the disposals account for disposal of the old machine showing any amount to be transferred to the statement of profit or loss, and the totals of the account.

Disposals £ £

Total		Total	

Select your entries from the following list: Balance b/d, Balance c/d, Bank, Depreciation charges, Machinery accumulated depreciation, Machinery at cost, Statement of financial position, Statement of profit or loss.

(iii) Is there a profit or a loss on disposal of the old machine?

Profit			Loss	

Task 2

This task is about recording period end adjustments.

You are working on the accounts of Anya Stanton, a sole trader, for the year ended 31 March 20-5.

(a) **(i)** Anya has an item of inventory for which she is unsure of the year-end valuation.

The cost of the item was £200, which, normally, Anya would mark-up by 50% for resale. However, the item is damaged and repairs will cost £50. Once repaired she will sell the item at a 20% discount.

What is the inventory valuation that should be included in the financial statements for this item? You may ignore VAT.

Inventory valuation	✔
£190	
£200	
£240	
£300	

(ii) Anya asks you to write off an irrecoverable debt. The customer is Exbury Developments and the amount of £175. You may ignore VAT.

Show the journal entry to write off this debt.

Journal number: 45	31 March 20-5	
Account name	**Debit** £	**Credit** £

Select your account entries from the following list: Allowance for doubtful receivables, Allowance for doubtful receivables adjustment, Exbury Developments, Irrecoverable debts, Receivables ledger control, Sales, Statement of profit or loss.

(b) You are considering Anya's commission income for the year ended 31 March 20-5.

- The balance of the commission income account at the beginning of the financial year is £600. This represents an accrual for commission income earned for the month of March 20-4.

- The cash book for the year shows receipts for commission income of £7,000.

- The commission income account has been adjusted for £750 commission income earned for the month of March 20-5. This amount was received and entered into the cash book on 7 April 20-5.

(i) Complete the following statements by calculating the required figure and selecting **one** option from each box.

One 1 April 20-4, the commission income account shows a | DEBIT / CREDIT |

balance of £ [   ].

On 31 March 20-5, the commission income account shows an adjustment for

| ACCRUED EXPENSES |
| ACCRUED INCOME |
| PREPAID EXPENSES |
| PREPAID INCOME |

of £ [   ].

(ii) Calculate the commission income for the year ended 31 March 20-5.

£ [   ]

(c) You are now considering Anya's selling expenses for the year ended 31 March 20-5.

- The cash book for the year shows bank payments for selling expenses of £6,420.

- The bank payments for the year include £525 for website services for the three months ended 30 April 20-5. Website services are classified under selling expenses.

Complete the selling expenses account for the year ended 31 March 20-5, showing the amount transferred to the statement of profit or loss. Dates are not required.

Select your account entries from the following list:

Accrued expenses, Accrued income, Balance b/d, Balance c/d, Bank, Prepaid expenses, Prepaid income, Selling expenses, Statement of profit or loss.

Selling expenses	£		£
		Accrued expenses reversal	360
Total		**Total**	

Task 3

This task is about producing, adjusting, checking and extending the trial balance.

(a) **(i)** Identify whether the following statements about extended trial balances are true or false.

Statement	True ✔	False ✔
The statement of profit or loss is an account in terms of double-entry bookkeeping.		
Owner's drawings are shown as a credit in the statement of profit or loss columns and a debit in the statement of financial position columns.		
The write-off of irrecoverable debts is shown as a credit to receivables ledger control in the adjustments columns.		
Interest on capital is an adjustment that may be found on a partnership extended trial balance.		

(ii) Denise runs a business which is not registered for VAT.

State the overall effect on the elements of the accounting equation for each of the following transactions.

Choose your options from the following list: Decrease, Increase, No effect.

Transaction	Assets	Liabilities	Capital
Denise pays extra capital into the business bank account in order to reduce the bank overdraft.			
Denise buys office equipment for use in the business on credit from Office Supplies Ltd.			

(b) You are reconciling the balance of payables ledger control account to the total of the account balances in payables ledger.

The balance of payables ledger control account is £33,943.

The total of the payables' account balances in payables ledger is £33,833.

Following an investigation, a number of errors have been discovered.

You are to identify the entries which need to be made in the relevant accounts to correct any errors that may have caused the difference between the two balances. Each error should have at least one entry next to it. If there is no overall effect, place a tick in the last column.

Errors	Payables ledger control account		Payables' accounts		No effect
	Debit £	Credit £	Debit £	Credit £	✔
An invoice for £750 (including VAT) from Dristan Ltd has been entered to the payables ledger account of Tristan Ltd.					
The total column of purchases returns day book has been overcast by £100.					
Discounts received from trade payables of £105 have been entered on the wrong side of payables ledger control account.					
A bank payment sent to Stella Ltd was for £560, but the amount that should have been paid is £650.					

(c) The trial balance for Vikki's business has been produced for the year ended 31 December 20-2. The debit column totals £146,391 and the credit column totals £146,038.

Prepare the entries to correct the following errors using the journal layout below. Dates and narratives are not required.

- The closing inventory has not been recorded in the accounts. It is valued at £4,170.

- Vikki withdrew £500 from the bank as drawings. This was recorded in drawings account but has been omitted from the bank.

- A bank payment for rent of £663 has been entered in the rent account as £636 (no VAT is applicable).

- Commission income of £120 has been entered twice in commission income account.

Tutorial note: where appropriate, use a single journal entry (one debit, one credit) rather than two entries.

Select your account names from the following list: Bank, Capital, Closing inventory: sfp*, Closing inventory: spl**, Commission income, Drawings, Inventory, Rent, Suspense.

      *   statement of financial position

    **   statement of profit or loss

Journal number: 28	31 December 20-2	
Account name	**Debit** £	**Credit** £

(d)   The extended trial balance (on the next page) for the year is part completed. **You are to** finish extending the trial balance, including calculation of the profit or loss – specify in the appropriate space in the first column whether it is a profit or a loss for the year.

Account name	Ledger balances		Adjustments		Statement of profit or loss		Statement of financial position	
	Dr £	**Cr £**	**Dr £**	**Cr £**	**Dr £**	**Cr £**	**Dr £**	**Cr £**
Allowance for doubtful receivables		2,100	250					
Allowance for doubtful receivables adjustment				250				
Bank	3,700						3,700	
Capital		40,000						40,000
Closing inventory			21,300	21,300				
Depreciation charges			2,750					
Machinery at cost	25,000						25,000	
Machinery accumulated depreciation		11,500		2,750				14,250
Office expenses	7,350			300	7,050			
Opening inventory	19,100							
Payables ledger control		11,400						11,400
Prepayment of expenses			300					
Purchases	76,200				76,200			
Receivables ledger control	30,950						30,950	
Sales		100,900				100,900		
Selling expenses	5,750				5,750			
VAT		2,150						2,150
*								
TOTAL	168,050	168,050	24,600	24,600				

* Select your entry from Profit for the year, Loss for the year.

Task 4

This task is about producing financial statements for sole traders and partnerships.

(a)   **(i)**   Identify whether each of the following transactions would lead to an increase, a decrease, or no change in the current assets of a business.

Transaction	Increase ✔	Decrease ✔	No change ✔
A receivable settles their account; the payment reduces the amount of the bank overdraft.			
Profit for the year.			
Owner takes goods for personal use.			
Owner transfers her computer into the business for use in the office.			

(ii)   Identify whether the following statements about partnership statements of financial position are true or false.

Statement	True ✔	False ✔
Interest on partners' drawings increases the profit to be shared amongst the partners.		
In most partnerships, each partner usually has a fixed capital account and a fluctuating current account.		

(b) The following information is required to answer tasks (b) (i) and (b) (ii).

Lena and Lucy run LL Supplies as a partnership. Their trial balance at 30 June 20-2 is shown below.

LL Supplies
Trial balance as at 30 June 20-2

	Dr £	Cr £
Accruals		550
Administration expenses	23,840	
Bank	8,340	
Capital account – Lena as at 1 July 20-1		40,000
Capital account – Lucy as at 1 July 20-1		17,500
Cash	270	
Closing inventory	8,050	8,050
Current account – Lena		1,390
Current account – Lucy	320	
Depreciation charges	6,820	
Discounts received		230
Drawings – Lena	12,020	
Drawings – Lucy	18,960	
Irrecoverable debts	400	
Motor vehicles at cost	52,500	
Motor vehicles accumulated depreciation		18,400
Opening inventory	7,240	
Prepayments	170	
Purchases	75,890	
Payables ledger control		7,200
Receivables ledger control	13,470	
Sales revenue		132,860
VAT		2,110
TOTAL	228,290	228,290

Additional information:

* Profits and losses are shared between Lena and Lucy in the ratio 55:45.

* Lucy works in the business and is entitled to a salary of £10,000. Lena is not entitled to a salary.

* Interest on capital, Lena £1,000, Lucy £450.

* Interest on drawings, Lena £240, Lucy £380.

(i) Complete the statement of profit or loss for LL Supplies for the year ended 30 June 20-2.

All numbers should be shown to the nearest £.

Profit figures should be shown as positive and loss figures should be shown as negative. All other figures should be shown as positive.

Select your entries from the following list:

Administration expenses, Capital account – Lena, Capital account – Lucy, Cash, Closing inventory, Current account – Lena, Current account – Lucy, Depreciation charges, Discounts received, Irrecoverable debts, Motor vehicles accumulated depreciation, Opening inventory, Purchases, VAT.

LL Supplies		
Statement of profit or loss for the year ended 30 June 20-2		
	£	£
Sales revenue		132,860
Less:		
Cost of sales		
Gross profit		
Add:		
Less:		
Total expenses		
Profit/Loss for the year		

(ii) Complete the following appropriation account for LL Supplies for the year ended 30 June 20-2.

All numbers should be shown to the nearest £.

Profit figures should be shown as positive and loss figures should be shown as negative. All other figures should be shown as positive.

Select your entries from the following list:

Capital, Drawings, Interest on drawings, Interest on capital, Partners' salaries.

Appropriation account for the year ended 30 June 20-2	Total £	Lena £	Lucy £
Profit/(loss) for the year			
Add			
Less appropriation of profits			
Profit available for distribution			
Profit share			
Lena			
Lucy			
Total profit distributed			

Task 5

This task is about accounting principles, qualities of useful financial information, and interpreting financial statements using profitability ratios.

(a)   **(i)**   Which **one** of the following best describes material misstatement?

Description	✔
When the accountant preparing the financial statements allows the influence of others to bias or override professional judgements.	
When users of financial statements do not receive information in time to make economic decisions.	
When the accounting principle of materiality has not been applied.	
When information contained in the financial statements is untrue and could influence the economic decisions of users.	

(ii)   Identify the enhancing qualitative characteristics described below.

Description	Characteristic
Financial information is presented clearly and concisely.	
Users of financial statements are assured that the information is faithfully represented.	

Select your characteristics from the following list: Comparability, Timeliness, Understandability, Verifiability.

(b)   Identify whether each of the statements about profitability ratios is true or false.

Statement	True ✔	False ✔
Return on capital employed measures profit for the year in relation to the capital employed by the business.		
Profitability ratios can be compared with ratios from a different business, or a different time period, or with industry standard ratios.		
The expenses/revenue percentage will often increase as the sales revenue of a business increases.		
Gross profit mark-up is a percentage profit based on the selling price.		

(c)   You have the following information about a business.

Statement of profit or loss extract	£
Sales revenue	420,250
Gross profit	98,340
Expenses	62,150
Profit/loss for the year	36,190
Statement of financial position extract	**£**
Non-current assets	310,640
Current assets	75,860
Current liabilities	62,190
Non-current liabilities	85,400
Capital	238,910

(i)   Calculate the following ratios (to TWO decimal places) from the information above.

Gross profit mark-up (%)	
Return on capital employed (%)	

(ii)   A business has calculated that its return on capital employed is lower this year than last year.

Identify whether the following statements about the decrease in the ratio are true or false.

Statement	True ✔	False ✔
The decrease could have been caused by additional capital being put into the business.		
The decrease could have been caused by paying off bank loans.		

Task 6

This task is about preparing accounting records from incomplete information.

(a) A trader has annual credit purchases of £130,340 including VAT from suppliers who allow 'net monthly' terms.

Identify which **one** of the following is most likely to be the balance of payables ledger control account at the end of the financial year?

£2,500	
£10,500	
£130,340	

(b) You have the following information about a business for its year ended 31 December 20-3:

- It is not registered for VAT.
- The trader operates with a gross profit mark-up of one-half.
- Inventory at 1 January 20-3 was £12,500.
- Inventory at 31 December 20-3 was £15,000.
- Sales of £75,000 were made.

Using this information, complete the following tasks:

(i) Calculate the cost of sales for the year ended 31 December 20-3.

£ [   ]

(ii) Calculate the value of purchases for the year ended 31 December 20-3.

£ [   ]

(iii) You compare the closing inventory figure of £15,000 with the results of the physical inventory count at the year-end. The total physical inventory value is £750 lower than your calculation.

Which **one** of the following could explain this?

	✔
An item has been omitted from the closing inventory figure.	
The trader has made drawings of goods during the year.	
Some purchases returns items being sent back on 31 December 20-3 have been included in the physical count.	
A computer bought for use in the office has been included in the physical count.	

(iv) Update the value of closing inventory to account for the difference above.

£ [   ]

(c)   You are preparing the accounting records of Imogen's business. The business is not registered for VAT.

The following information relates to the financial year ended 31 March 20-6:

Bank receipts and payments	£
Amounts from credit customers	67,031
Amounts to credit suppliers	27,846
Drawings	12,500
Office expenses	19,361
Bank interest paid	247

Balances at:	31 March 20-5 £	31 March 20-6 £
Receivables	8,216	9,047
Payables	4,367	4,498
Closing inventory	4,221	4,864
Bank	Overdrawn 3,219	At bank 1,246

You are also told that:

•   all sales are on credit terms

•   sales totalled £68,422 for the year

For parts (i), (ii) and (iii) select your account names from the following list:

Allowance for doubtful receivables, Allowance for doubtful receivables adjustment, Balance b/d, Balance c/d, Bank, Bank interest paid, Capital, Cash purchases, Closing inventory, Drawings, Irrecoverable debts, Office expenses, Opening inventory, Payables ledger control, Purchases, Receivables ledger control, Sales.

(i)   Using the information supplied, prepare the payables ledger control account for the year in order to find the amount of purchases on credit.

Payables ledger control			
Account name	**£**	**Account name**	**£**
Total		Total	

(ii) During the year, a customer was declared bankrupt and the amount has been written off in full.

Using the information supplied, prepare the receivables ledger control account for the year in order to find the amount written off.

Receivables ledger control			
Account name	**£**	**Account name**	**£**
Total		Total	

(iii) Using the information supplied, prepare a summarised bank account for the year in order to find the amount of cash purchases.

Bank			
Account name	**£**	**Account name**	**£**
Total		Total	

Practice assessment 3

Assessment information

- This practice assessment contains **6 tasks** and you should attempt to complete **every** task.

- Each task is independent. You will not need to refer to your answers from previous tasks.

- Read every task carefully to make sure you understand what is required.

- Where the date is relevant, it is given in the task data.

- Both minus signs and brackets can be used to indicate negative numbers **unless** task instructions state otherwise.

- You must use a full stop to indicate a decimal point. For example, write 100.57, **not** 100,57 or 10057.

- You may use a comma to indicate a number in the thousands, but you don't have to. For example, 10000 and 10,000 are both acceptable.

Task 1

This task is about using day books and accounting for and monitoring non-current assets.

(a) **(i)** Identify whether the following statements are true or false.

Statement	True ✔	False ✔
Day books are used in a manual accounting system to summarise transactions before they are entered in the ledgers.		
Non-current assets are usually tangible items that are used in the production of goods or services, and have a life span of more than one year.		
In a manual accounting system, capital introduced into the business does not require an entry in a book of prime entry.		

(ii) A business wishes to buy a high-value non-current asset.

Which **two** of the following statements are correct?

Statement	✔
The capital expenditure must fit in with the business's plans and budgets.	
The method of funding the non-current asset must be arranged prior to purchase.	
The decision to buy the non-current asset is taken by the person who will use the asset.	

(iii) Complete the following statement about depreciation of non-current assets.

The carrying amount of a non-current asset is …

	✔
the cost of the asset less its residual value	
the cost of the asset less its depreciation to date	
the original cost of the asset	

(b) You are an Accounts Assistant at Toynton Trading. The business is registered for VAT and has a financial year-end of 31 March.

On 26 March 20-0, Toynton Trading received an invoice for a PHX laptop computer bought for the sales manager. An extract from this invoice is shown below:

Item	Total
	£
PHX Laptop computer	740.00
Next day delivery	10.00
Printer cartridge	20.00
VAT @ 20%	154.00
Total	924.00

The following information relates to the sale of a car no longer required by the business:

Description	2.0 litre car PT17 PZV
Date of sale	14 March 20-0
Selling price	£7,500.00 bank transfer received

- Toynton Trading has a policy of capitalising expenditure over £500.

- Computer equipment is depreciated at 30% on a straight-line basis assuming no residual value.

- Vehicles are depreciated at 25% on a diminishing balance basis.

- A full year's depreciation is applied in the year of acquisition and none in the year of disposal.

(i)   Complete the extract from the non-current asset register for:

- any acquisitions of non-current assets during the year ended 31 March 20-0

- any disposals of non-current assets during the year ended 31 March 20-0

- depreciation for the year ended 31 March 20-0

All figures should be shown to two decimal places.

Extract from non-current assets register

Description/serial no	Acquisition date	Cost £	Depreciation charges £	Carrying amount £	Disposal proceeds £	Disposal date
Computer equipment						
PHX Laser printer	15/12/20-7	1,200.00				
Year-end 31/03/20-8			360.00	840.00		
Year-end 31/03/20-9			360.00	480.00		
Year-end 31/03/20-0						
PHX Laptop computer	26/03/20-0					
Year-end 31/03/20-0						
Vehicles						
PT17 PZV	20/05/20-7	16,000.00				
Year-end 31/03/20-8			4,000.00	12,000.00		
Year-end 31/03/20-9			3,000.00	9,000.00		
Year-end 31/03/20-0						
PT68 ZPE	19/11/20-8	14,400.00				
Year-end 31/03/20-9			3,600.00	10,800.00		
Year-end 31/03/20-0						

(ii) Complete the disposals account for vehicle PT17 PZV showing the amount to be transferred to the statement of profit or loss, and the totals of the account. Show your answer to two decimal places.

Disposals	£		£
Total		**Total**	

Select your entries from the following list: Balance b/d, Balance c/d, Bank, Depreciation expense, Statement of financial position, Statement of profit or loss, Vehicles Accumulated depreciation, Vehicles at cost.

(iii) Complete the journal entry for the depreciation charge for all of the computer equipment for the year ended 31 March 20-0. Show your answer to two decimal places.

Journal number: 72	31 March 20-0	
Account name	**Debit**	**Credit**
	£	£

Select your entries from the following list: Balance b/d, Balance c/d, Bank, Computer equipment at cost, Computer equipment accumulated depreciation, Depreciation expense, Statement of financial position, Statement of profit or loss.

Task 2

This task is about recording period end adjustments.

You are working on the accounts of Kate Kassir, who sells garden supplies, for the year ended 30 June 20-5. Her business is not registered for VAT.

(a) **(i)** Kate provides you with the following year-end valuations for each group of inventory that she sells:

	Cost £	Selling price £
Seeds	3,100	2,900
Fertilisers	4,540	7,120
Tools	8,780	13,480
Total	16,420	23,860

What valuation for closing inventory will you use in her financial statements?

Valuation	✔
£16,220	
£16,420	
£23,700	
£23,860	

(ii) State which accounting principle best relates to your valuation of Kate's inventory.

Accounting principle	✔
Accruals	
Business entity	
Consistency	
Going concern	
Materiality	
Money measurement	
Prudence	

(iii) Kate asks you to write off an irrecoverable debt. The customer is Digger Jo and the amount is £125.

Show the journal entry to write off this debt.

Journal number: 32		30 June 20-5
Account name	**Debit** £	**Credit** £

Select your account entries from the following list: Allowance for doubtful receivables, Allowance for doubtful receivables adjustment, Digger Jo, Irrecoverable debts, Receivables ledger control, Sales, Statement of profit or loss.

(b) Kate sublets part of her premises to another business.

You are considering rent received for the year ended 30 June 20-5.

• The balance of the rent received account at the beginning of the financial year is £650. This represents a prepayment by the tenant of rent for July 20-4.

• The cash book for the year shows receipts for rent of £7,500.

• The rent received account has been adjusted for £700 rent due for the month of June 20-5. This amount was received and entered into the cash book on 8 July 20-5.

(i) Complete the following statements by calculating the required figure and selecting **one** option from each box.

On 1 July 20-4, the rent received account shows a | DEBIT / CREDIT |

balance of £ [   ] .

On 30 June 20-5, the rent received account shows an adjustment for

| ACCRUED EXPENSES
ACCRUED INCOME
PREPAID EXPENSES
PREPAID INCOME | of £ [   ] .

(ii) Calculate the rent received for the year ended 30 June 20-5.

£ [   ]

(c) You are now considering Kate's shop expenses for the year ended 30 June 20-5.

- The cash book for the year shows bank payments for shop expenses of £4,680.

- The bank payments for the year include £480 for website services for the three months ended 31 August 20-5. Website services are classified as shop expenses.

Complete the shop expenses account for the year ended 30 June 20-5 and show the amount transferred to the statement of profit or loss. Dates are not required.

Select your account entries from the following list:

Accrued expenses, Accrued income, Balance b/d, Balance c/d, Bank, Prepaid expenses, Prepaid income, Shop expenses, Statement of profit or loss.

Shop expenses

	£		£
Prepaid expenses reversal	120		
Total		Total	

Task 3

This task is about producing, adjusting, checking and extending the trial balance.

(a)   **(i)**   A trial balance will disclose certain errors.

Identify whether each of the errors listed below will be disclosed or will not be disclosed by a trial balance. Ignore VAT.

Error	Error disclosed by the trial balance ✔	Error not disclosed by the trial balance ✔
A bank payment for £284 has been debited in the payables ledger to John Peters instead of Peter Johns.		
The balance of sales account has been calculated incorrectly.		
A bank payment for vehicle repairs has been debited to vehicles account.		
Drawings of £150 have been recorded in bank account but not in drawings account.		

(ii)   Matt runs a business which is not registered for VAT.

State the overall effect on the elements of the accounting equation for each of the following transactions.

Choose your options from the following list: Decrease, Increase, No effect.

Transaction	Assets	Liabilities	Capital
Matt takes out a bank loan to buy a new computer for use in the business.			
Matt makes a bank payment to a credit supplier, which increases his overdraft.			

(b) You are reconciling the balance of Evie's receivables ledger control account to the total of the account balances in receivables ledger.

The balance of receivables ledger control account is £25,362.

The total of the receivables account balances in receivables ledger is £25,271.

Following an investigation, a number of errors have been discovered.

You are to identify the entries which need to be made in the relevant accounts to correct any errors that may have caused the difference between the two balances. Each error should have at least one entry next to it. If there is no overall effect, place a tick in the last column.

Errors	Receivables ledger control account		Receivables accounts		No effect
	Debit £	Credit £	Debit £	Credit £	✔
The account of Manners & Co, £175, has been written off in receivables ledger, but has not been recorded in receivables ledger control account.					
The total column of sales returns day book has been overcast by £200.					
Discounts allowed to trade receivables of £58 have been entered on the wrong side of receivables ledger control account.					
A bank payment for £250 from Quin Ltd has been entered in the receivables ledger account of Quinn & Co.					

(c) The ledger columns of the extended trial balance for Alexandra Lukac's business have been produced for the year ended 31 December 20-3.

The debit column totals £481,261 and the credit column totals £480,261. A suspense account has been opened.

You are to correct the following errors by entering adjustments in the extended trial balance:

- A bank payment for rent for £1,200 has been reversed in the accounts (no VAT is applicable).

- The total column in the purchases daybook has been overcast by £1,000.

- The closing inventory has not been recorded in the accounts. It is valued at £6,490.

- Alexandra paid additional capital of £2,000 into her business. This was recorded in the cash book, but not in her capital account.

Trial balance for Alexandra Lukac as at 31 December 20-3				
Account name	**Ledger balances**		**Adjustments**	
	Dr £	**Cr £**	**Dr £**	**Cr £**
Administration expenses	53,941			
Bank	5,200			
Capital		56,500		
Depreciation charges	15,150			
Drawings	12,185			
Irrecoverable debts	395			
Machinery at cost	158,500			
Machinery accumulated depreciation		42,300		
Office expenses	31,046			
Opening inventory	5,212			
Payables ledger control		11,147		
Purchases	146,038			
Receivables ledger control	20,868			
Rent	10,380			
Sales		365,242		
Selling expenses	22,346			
VAT		5,072		
Closing inventory: Statement of financial position				
Closing inventory: Statement of profit or loss				
Suspense		1,000		
TOTAL	481,261	481,261		

(d) You are working on the trial balance of Linda Goode as at 31 December 20-3.

An extract of the trial balance is shown below and you are to record a number of adjustments to the trial balance:

- Prepaid income is £500.

- Accrued expenses are £425.

- Depreciation expense is £2,250.

- Disposal of non-current assets has resulted in a loss of £850.

- Irrecoverable debts are £345.

- Discounts received are £164.

You are to complete the trial balance extract which follows.

Extract of the trial balance of Linda Goode as at 31 December 20-3		
	Dr £	Cr £
Prepaid income		
Accrued expenses		
Depreciation expense		
Disposal of non-current assets		
Irrecoverable debts		
Discounts received		

Task 4

This task is about producing financial statements for sole traders and partnerships.

(a) **(i)** Identify whether the following statements are true or false.

Statement	True ✔	False ✔
Partnership profits are always split equally between the partners.		
In a partnership, a partner's capital account is normally fixed and only alters if permanent capital changes.		
In a partnership, a partner's current account is credited with interest on drawings.		
The accounting rules for a partnership are often set out in a partnership agreement.		

(ii) In a partnership appropriation account, identify which **one** of the following statements describes the profit available for distribution.

Statement	✔
Profit for the year + interest on drawings – partner's salary + interest on capital	
Profit for the year – interest on drawings – partner's salary – interest on capital	
Profit for the year + interest on drawings – partner's salary – interest on capital	
Profit for the year + interest on drawings + partner's salary – interest on capital	

(iii) Complete the following statement.

The purpose of a statement of profit or loss is to show ...	✔
the profitability of the business.	
the cash position of the business.	
that there are no errors in the accounting system.	
the assets and liabilities of the business at a given date.	

(b) Phoebe runs a shop selling parts for cars and vans. She is a sole trader and her year-end is 31 March 20-1.

You are given her trial balance at 31 March 20-1.

Phoebe's Motor Parts

Trial balance as at 31 March 20-1

	Dr £	Cr £
Bank	31,164	
Capital at 1 April 20-0		60,500
Closing inventory	12,035	12,035
Depreciation charges	2,050	
Disposal of non-current assets		549
Drawings	23,550	
Irrecoverable debts	268	
Opening inventory	11,392	
Purchases	68,217	
Payables ledger control		10,157
Receivables ledger control	10,047	
Sales		145,298
Shop expenses	48,362	
Shop fittings accumulated depreciation		6,870
Shop fittings at cost	30,200	
VAT		1,876
TOTAL	237,285	237,285

(i) Phoebe's statement of profit or loss has already been calculated and her profit for the year is £27,593.

An adjustment needs to be made for car parts taken by Phoebe during the year for repairs to her private car. The cost of these was £360 including VAT.

Complete the journal entry to account for this.

Select your account names from the following list: Bank, Capital, Drawings, Purchases, Sales, Shop expenses, VAT.

Journal number: 32		31 March 20-1	
	Debit **£**	**Credit** **£**	

(ii) After the journal entry has been processed, what is the revised profit for the year?

£ ⬚

(iii) Complete Phoebe's capital account for the year.

Select your account names from the following list: Balance b/d, Balance c/d, Bank, Drawings, Profit for the year, Purchases, Sales, VAT.

Capital			
Account name	**£**	**Account name**	**£**
Total		Total	

(iv) Using the figures in the trial balance, complete an extract of Phoebe's Statement of financial position. (Note you are completing the SFP down to the net assets figure.)

Select your entries from the following list: Bank, Capital, Depreciation charges, Disposal of non-current asset, Drawings, Inventory, Irrecoverable debts, Purchases, Sales, Shop expenses, Shop fittings accumulated depreciation, Shop fittings at cost, Trade payables, Trade receivables, VAT.

Phoebe's Motor Parts Statement of financial position as at 31 March 20-1	Cost £	Accumulated depreciation £	Carrying amount £
Non-current assets			
Current assets			
Total current assets			
Current liabilities			
Total current liabilities			
Net current liabilities			
Net assets			

Task 5

This task is about accounting principles, qualities of useful financial information, and interpreting financial statements using profitability ratios.

(a) **(i)** Identify the accounting principle being described by each of the following statements.

Statement	Accounting principle
When preparing financial statements for a business, the presumption is that it will continue to trade in the foreseeable future.	
The private house of the owner of the business is not recorded on the statement of financial position of the business.	
The value of goods purchased for resale but not yet paid for at the year-end is included in purchases for the year.	
Low value non-current assets are expensed to the statement of profit or loss.	

Select from the following list:

Accounting principle
Accruals
Business entity
Consistency
Going concern
Materiality
Money measurement
Prudence

(ii) Identify which **one** of the following groups is considered to be the primary users of financial statements.

Groups	✔
Investors, employees, managers of the business	
Lenders, other creditors, customers	
Lenders, existing and potential investors, other creditors	
Customers, lenders, potential investors	

(b) Identify whether each of the statements about profitability ratios is true or false.

Statement	True ✔	False ✔
A gross profit margin of 20% is the equivalent of a gross profit mark-up of 25%.		
Professional scepticism when interpreting financial information includes having a questioning mind and making a critical assessment.		
An increase in the amount of mark-up applied to goods purchased for resale will result in a lower gross profit.		
Comparisons of ratios can be made with a different business, a different time period, and an industry standard.		

(c) You have the following information about a business.

Statement of profit or loss extract	£
Sales revenue	450,390
Gross profit	185,640
Profit/loss for the year	22,380
Statement of financial position extract	**£**
Current liabilities	53,170
Non-current liabilities	42,680
Capital	120,420

(i) Calculate the following ratios (to TWO decimal places) from the information above.

Net profit margin (%)	
Return on capital employed (%)	

(ii) The selling expenses/revenue percentage for last year was 7.6%. This year the selling expenses/revenue percentage is calculated to be 9.8%.

Identify whether the following statements about the increase in the ratio are true or false.

Statement	True ✔	False ✔
The increase could have been caused by sales revenue rising during the year.		
The increase could have been caused by higher expenditure on selling expenses during the year.		
The increase in the current year's percentage shows improvement when compared with the previous year.		

(d) Identify what effect (if any) each of the following scenarios may have on the ratios stated. Each scenario is independent.

Scenario 1

A business has reduced its selling prices, whilst maintaining the quality of its products.

	Increase ✔	Unchanged ✔	Decrease ✔
Return on capital employed			
Cost of sales/revenue percentage			

Scenario 2

A business has bought new non-current assets to replace old and fully depreciated assets. Production will continue at current levels.

	Increase ✔	Unchanged ✔	Decrease ✔
Gross profit margin			
Net profit margin			

Task 6

This task is about preparing accounting records from incomplete information.

(a)   A trader has annual sales to credit customers of £140,250 including VAT and has a policy of allowing credit customers to settle their accounts six weeks after the sale is made.

Identify which **one** of the following is most likely to be the balance of receivables ledger control account at the end of the financial year?

£13,500	
£16,200	
£116,800	

(b)   A business has printed out an inventory report at the end of the financial year. This shows that the balance of product QXP was 690 units with a value of £10 per unit. A physical inventory check shows that 675 units of product QXP are held in the warehouse.

Complete the following statement by selecting **one** of the options below for each gap.

If the closing inventory figure reported by the accounting software is higher than the physical inventory check, this could lead to gross profit being .... [GAP 1] .... and current assets being .... [GAP 2] ....

GAP 1
overstated
understated

GAP 2
overstated
understated

(c)   Chrissy is a sole trader who is registered for VAT. You are preparing her accounts for the year ended 31 December 20-9.

You have the following information for the year:

•   Sales including VAT £135,480.

•   Chrissy uses a gross profit margin of 35%.

•   Purchases (excluding VAT) for the year were £73,420.

•   The inventory as at 1 January 20-9 was £8,390.

(i)   Calculate the value of the sales net of VAT.

£ [   ]

(ii)   Calculate the cost of sales for the year.

£ [   ]

(iii)   Calculate the gross profit for the year.

£ [   ]

(iv)   Calculate the inventory as at 31 December 20-9.

£ [   ]

(v)   Chrissy uses an administration expenses account for all of her business expenses.

You have the following information for the year:

Administration expenses of £140 net of VAT were prepaid at 1 January 20-9.

The day book summary for administration expenses for the year shows:

Net £	VAT £	Total £
23,610	4,722	28,332

Administration expenses of £210 net of VAT were accrued at 31 December 20-9.

Using the information above, prepare the administration account for the year in order to show the amount to be transferred to the statement of profit or loss.

Select your account names from the following list: Accrued expenses, Accrued expenses reversal, Administration expenses day book, Balance b/d, Balance c/d, Bank, Prepaid expenses, Prepaid expenses reversal, Statement of profit or loss.

Administration expenses			
Account name	**£**	**Account name**	**£**
Total		Total	

(vi)   Administration expenses is the only expense for the statement of profit or loss.

Calculate the profit for the year ended 31 December 20-9.

£ [   ]

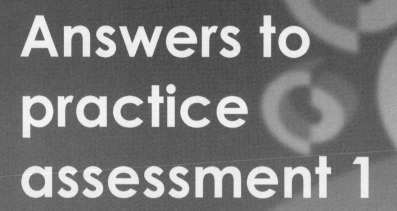

Answers to practice assessment 1

Task 1

(a) **(i)**

Statement	Option
A list of credit sales made, compiled from invoices issued, is recorded initially in the …	Sales day book
Discounts from suppliers for prompt payment of invoices are recorded initially in the …	Discounts received day book

(ii)

Item	Understated	Overstated	No effect
Net profit	✔		
Current assets			✔
Current liabilities			✔
Non-current assets	✔		

(b)

Accounting principle	
Prudence	✔
Business entity	
Going concern	
Materiality	
Accruals	✔

(c) **(i)** £800 depreciation charge

Machinery at cost	£		£
Balance b/d	25,000	Balance c/d	31,000
Bank	6,000		
Total	31,000	**Total**	31,000

Machinery depreciation charges	£		£
Balance b/d	5,000	Statement of profit or loss	5,800
Machinery accumulated depreciation	800		
Total	5,800	**Total**	5,800

Machinery accumulated depreciation   £   £

Balance c/d	10,800	Balance b/d	10,000
		Machinery depreciation charges	800
Total	**10,800**	**Total**	**10,800**

(ii)

It shows the carrying amount of each machine	✔
It proves legal ownership of each machine	
It shows how much each machine will be sold for when it is disposed	
It shows when it is time to replace each machine	

(iii)

Debit Disposals; Credit Bank	
Debit Vehicle at cost; Credit Bank	
Debit Bank; Credit Disposals	✔
Debit Bank; Credit Vehicles at cost	

Task 2

(a)   (i)

Item	Included in valuation	Not included in valuation
Purchase cost of wood	✔	
Labour costs to make the furniture	✔	
Selling costs to market the furniture		✔
Costs of storage of finished furniture		✔

(ii)

Item	No effect	Understated	Overstated
Assets		✔	
Profit		✔	

(b)

Rent paid account			
	£		£
Prepaid expenses reversal	500	Prepaid expenses	1,400
Cash book	7,500	Statement of profit or loss	6,600
Total	8,000	Total	8,000

(c)

Journal number: 564	30 June 20-2	
Account name	Debit	Credit
	£	£
Irrecoverable debts	225	
Receivables ledger control		225
Allowance for doubtful receivables	25	
Allowance for doubtful receivables adjustment		25

Task 3

(a) (i)

Statement	Option
Irrecoverable debts are ...	an expense item
A bank overdraft is ...	a current liability

(ii)

Error	Error disclosed by the trial balance	Error not disclosed by the trial balance
A bank payment for telephone expenses has been recorded on the debit side of both the cash book and telephone expenses account.	✔	
A sales invoice has been omitted from all accounting records.		✔
The balance of purchases returns account has been calculated incorrectly.	✔	
A bank payment of £85 for stationery has been recorded as £58 in both accounts.		✔

(b) **(i)** £134.64 debit

(ii)

Bank reconciliation statement as at 30 June 20-2	£
Closing bank statement balance	(230.56)
Less	
Kelly Ltd	108.24
Add	
Gomez & Co	473.44
Closing cash book balance	134.64

(c)

Journal number: 176	30 June 20-3	
Account name	Debit £	Credit £
Closing inventory: sfp	6,290	
Closing inventory: spl		6,290
Rent paid	1,500	
Bank		1,500
Office expenses	90	
Suspense		90
Office equipment	850	
Suspense		850

(d)

Account name	Ledger balances		Adjustments		Statement of profit or loss		Statement of financial position	
	Dr £	Cr £	Dr £	Cr £	Dr £	Cr £	Dr £	Cr £
Accrual of wages				230				230
Bank	9,420						9,420	
Capital		35,000		10,500				45,500
Closing inventory			9,450	9,450		9,450	9,450	
Depreciation charges	4,700				4,700			
Drawings			10,500				10,500	
Expenses	26,081			346	25,735			
Machinery at cost	23,500						23,500	
Machinery accumulated depreciation		7,920						7,920
Opening inventory	8,190				8,190			
Payables ledger control		7,368						7,368
Prepayment of expenses			346				346	
Purchases	58,484				58,484			
Receivables ledger control	13,378						13,378	
Rent receivable		2,765				2,765		
Sales		117,784				117,784		
Wages	27,084		230		27,314			
Profit for the year					5,576			5,576
TOTAL	170,837	170,837	20,526	20,526	129,999	129,999	66,594	66,594

Task 4

(a) **(i)**

Transaction	Increase	Decrease	No change
Owner arranges a bank overdraft			✔
Loss for the year		✔	
Owner takes goods for personal use		✔	
Owner transfers her computer into the business	✔		

(ii)

Statement	True	False
The statement of financial position shows the year-end balances on each partner's capital and current account.	✔	
A debit balance on a partner's current account means that the partner has drawn out more than his/her share of the profit.	✔	

(b)   (i)

Sarton Supplies Statement of profit or loss for the year ended 31 March 20-1		
	£	£
Sales revenue		95,320
Less:		
Opening inventory	5,150	
Purchases	45,930	
Closing inventory	6,090	
Cost of sales		44,990
Gross profit		50,330
Add:		
Discounts received		160
Less:		
Administration expenses	16,210	
Depreciation charges	4,750	
Irrecoverable debts	120	
Other expenses	9,120	
Total expenses		30,200
Profit/Loss for the year		20,290

(ii)

Appropriation account for the year ended 31 March 20-1	Total £	Sara £	Toni £
Profit/(loss) for the year	20,290		
Add			
Interest on drawings	330	225	105
Less appropriation of profits			
Partners' salaries	12,000	-	12,000
Interest on capital	1,425	750	675
Profit available for distribution	7,195		
Profit share			
Sara	4,317		
Toni	2,878		
Total profit distributed	7,195		

Task 5

(a) (i)

Description	Accounting principle
Inventory is valued at the lower of cost and net realisable value.	Prudence
Income and expenses are matched to relate to the same goods and services and the same accounting period.	Accruals
Depreciation of non-current assets is made at 10% a year, using the straight-line method.	Consistency
Financial statements are prepared on the basis that the business will continue to trade in the foreseeable future.	Going concern

(ii)

Description	Characteristic
Financial information is useful to the users of financial statements.	Relevance
Users of financial statements receive information quickly enough to enable decisions to be made.	Timeliness

(b)

Statement	True	False
Profitability ratios measure profit against the denominators of inventory, trade receivables or trade payables.		✔
Businesses use profitability ratios to aid control, decision-making and planning of the business.	✔	
Profitability ratios can highlight symptoms within a business, but the cause will need to be investigated.	✔	
The gross profit margin for a food supermarket and a furniture retailer should be very similar.		✔

(c)   (i)

Gross profit margin (%)	22.68%
Return on capital employed (%)	19.26%

(ii)

Statement	True	False
The decrease could have been caused by sales revenue rising during the year.	✔	
The decrease could have been caused by reduced revenue expenditure during the year.	✔	

Task 6

(a)

£6,400	✔
£9,200	
£110,380	

(b)   (i)   £46,380

(ii)   £12,050

(iii)

A high value item has not been included in the closing inventory figure	✔
The trader has made drawings of goods during the year	
Some inventory items have been taken for use in the office	
Some sales returns items have been missed in the physical count	

(iv)   £12,550

(c) **(i)**

Receivables ledger control			
Account name	**£**	**Account name**	**£**
Balance c/d	18,275	Sales returns	3,120
Sales	160,800	Bank	152,490
		Balance c/d	23,465
Total	179,075	Total	179,075

(ii)

VAT control			
Account name	**£**	**Account name**	**£**
Sales returns	520	Balance b/d	2,140
Purchases day book	16,400	Sales day book	26,800
Bank	7,245	Cash sales	1,720
Balance c/d	6,495		
Total	30,660	Total	30,660

Answers to practice assessment 2

Task 1

(a)   (i)

Statement	Option
Credit notes received for goods sent back to suppliers are recorded initially in the …	Purchases returns day book
The book of prime entry for cash purchases is the …	Cash book

(ii)

Items of expenditure	Capital expenditure	Revenue expenditure
Cost of a new vehicle	✔	
Cost of insurance for vehicles		✔
Cost of an extension to the premises	✔	
Cost of delivery for a new machine	✔	

(iii)

Depreciation charge for the year is recorded in the …	Statement of profit or loss
The carrying amount of a non-current asset is recorded in the …	Statement of financial position

(b)   (i)   £ 350   depreciation charge

Computers at cost   £   £

Balance b/d	9,500	Balance c/d	11,750
Bank	2,250		
Total	11,750	**Total**	11,750

Computers depreciation charges   £   £

Balance b/d	2,000	Statement of profit or loss	2,350
Computers accumulated depreciation	350		
Total	2,350	**Total**	2,350

Computers accumulated depreciation   £   £

Balance c/d	4,350	Balance b/d	4,000
		Computers depreciation charges	350
Total	**4,350**	**Total**	**4,350**

(ii)

Disposals   £   £

Machinery at cost	4,000	Machinery accumulated depreciation	2,400
		Machinery at cost	1,000
		Statement of profit or loss	600
Total	**4,000**	**Total**	**4,000**

(iii)   Loss

Task 2

(a)   **(i)**

Inventory valuation	
£190	✔
£200	
£240	
£300	

(ii)

Journal number: 45	**31 March 20-5**	
Account name	**Debit**	**Credit**
	£	**£**
Irrecoverable debts	175	
Receivables ledger control		175

(b) **(i)** One 1 April 20-4, the commission income account shows a **DEBIT** balance of £**600**.

On 31 March 20-5, the commission income account shows an adjustment for **ACCRUED INCOME** of £**750**.

(ii) £7,150

(c)

Selling expenses	£		£
Bank	6,420	Accrued expenses reversal	360
		Prepaid expenses	175
		Statement of profit or loss	5,885
Total	**6,420**	**Total**	**6,420**

Task 3
(a) **(i)**

Statement	True	False
The statement of profit or loss is an account in terms of double-entry bookkeeping.	✔	
Owner's drawings are shown as a credit in the statement of profit or loss columns and a debit in the statement of financial position columns.		✔
The write-off of irrecoverable debts is shown as a credit to receivables ledger control in the adjustments columns.	✔	
Interest on capital is an adjustment that may be found on a partnership extended trial balance.	✔	

(ii)

Transaction	Assets	Liabilities	Capital
Denise pays extra capital into the business bank account in order to reduce the bank overdraft.	No effect	Decrease	Increase
Denise buys office equipment for use in the business on credit from Office Supplies Ltd.	Increase	Increase	No effect

(b)

Errors	Payables ledger control account		Payables' accounts		No effect
	Debit £	**Credit** £	**Debit** £	**Credit** £	✔
An invoice for £750 (including VAT) from Dristan Ltd has been entered to the payables ledger account of Tristan Ltd.					✔
The total column of purchases returns day book has been overcast by £100.		100			
Discounts received from trade payables of £105 have been entered on the wrong side of payables ledger control account.	210				
A bank payment sent to Stella Ltd was for £560, but the amount that should have been paid is £650.					✔

(c)

Journal number: 28	31 December 20-2	
Account name	**Debit** £	**Credit** £
Closing inventory: sfp	4,170	
Closing inventory: spl		4,170
Suspense	500	
Bank		500
Rent	27	
Suspense		27
Commission income	120	
Suspense		120

(d)

Account name	Ledger balances		Adjustments		Statement of profit or loss		Statement of financial position	
	Dr £	Cr £	Dr £	Cr £	Dr £	Cr £	Dr £	Cr £
Allowance for doubtful receivables		2,100	250					1,850
Allowance for doubtful receivables adjustment				250		250		
Bank	3,700						3,700	
Capital		40,000						40,000
Closing inventory			21,300	21,300		21,300	21,300	
Depreciation charges			2,750		2,750			
Machinery at cost	25,000						25,000	
Machinery accumulated depreciation		11,500		2,750				14,250
Office expenses	7,350			300	7,050			
Opening inventory	19,100				19,100			
Payables ledger control		11,400						11,400
Prepayment of expenses			300				300	
Purchases	76,200				76,200			
Receivables ledger control	30,950						30,950	
Sales		100,900				100,900		
Selling expenses	5,750				5,750			
VAT		2,150						2,150
Profit for the year					11,600			11,600
TOTAL	168,050	168,050	24,600	24,600	122,450	122,450	81,250	81,250

Task 4

(a) **(i)**

Transaction	Increase	Decrease	No change
A receivable settles their account; the payment reduces the amount of the bank overdraft.		✔	
Profit for the year.			✔
Owner takes goods for personal use.		✔	
Owner transfers her computer into the business for use in the office.			✔

(ii)

Statement	True	False
Interest on partners' drawings increases the profit to be shared amongst the partners.	✔	
In most partnerships, each partner usually has a fixed capital account and a fluctuating current account.	✔	

(b) **(i)**

LL Supplies		
Statement of profit or loss for the year ended 30 June 20-2		
	£	£
Sales revenue		132,860
Less:		
Opening inventory	7,240	
Purchases	75,890	
Closing inventory	8,050	
Cost of sales		75,080
Gross profit		57,780
Add:		
Discounts received		230
Less:		
Administration expenses	23,840	
Depreciation charges	6,820	
Irrecoverable debts	400	
Total expenses		31,060
Profit/Loss for the year		26,950

(ii)

Appropriation account for the year ended 30 June 20-2	Total £	Lena £	Lucy £
Profit/(loss) for the year	26,950		
Add			
Interest on drawings	620	240	380
Less appropriation of profits			
Partners' salaries	10,000	0	10,000
Interest on capital	1,450	1,000	450
Profit available for distribution	16,120		
Profit share			
Lena	8,866		
Lucy	7,254		
Total profit distributed	16,120		

Task 5

(a)   (i)

Description	
When the accountant preparing the financial statements allows the influence of others to bias or override professional judgements.	
When users of financial statements do not receive information in time to make economic decisions.	
When the accounting principle of materiality has not been applied.	
When information contained in the financial statements is untrue and could influence the economic decisions of users.	✔

(ii)

Description	Characteristic
Financial information is presented clearly and concisely.	Understandability
Users of financial statements are assured that the information is faithfully represented.	Verifiability

(b)

Statement	True	False
Return on capital employed measures profit for the year in relation to the capital employed by the business.	✔	
Profitability ratios can be compared with ratios from a different business, or a different time period, or with industry standard ratios.	✔	
The expenses/revenue percentage will often increase as the sales revenue of a business increases.		✔
Gross profit mark-up is a percentage profit based on the selling price.		✔

(c) **(i)**

Gross profit mark-up (%)	30.55%
Return on capital employed (%)	11.16%

(ii)

Statement	True	False
The decrease could have been caused by additional capital being put into the business.	✔	
The decrease could have been caused by paying off bank loans.		✔

Task 6

(a)

£2,500	
£10,500	✔
£130,340	

(b) **(i)** £50,000

(ii) £52,500

(iii)

An item has been omitted from the closing inventory figure.	
The trader has made drawings of goods during the year.	✔
Some purchases returns items being sent back on 31 December 20-3 have been included in the physical count.	
A computer bought for use in the office has been included in the physical count.	

(iv) £14,250

(c) **(i)**

Payables ledger control			
Account name	£	Account name	£
Bank	27,846	Balance b/d	4,367
Balance c/d	4,498	Purchases	27,977
Total	32,344	Total	32,344

(ii)

Receivables ledger control			
Account name	£	Account name	£
Balance b/d	8,216	Bank	67,031
Sales	68,422	Irrecoverable debts	560
		Balance c/d	9,047
Total	76,638	Total	76,638

(iii)

Bank			
Account name	£	Account name	£
Receivables ledger control	67,031	Balance b/d	3,219
		Payables ledger control	27,846
		Drawings	12,500
		Office expenses	19,361
		Bank interest paid	247
		Cash purchases	2,612
		Balance c/d	1,246
Total	67,031	Total	67,031

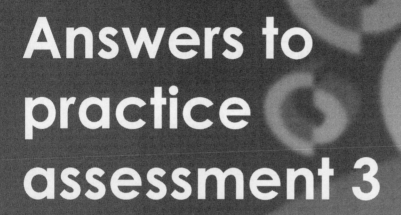

Answers to practice assessment 3

Task 1

(a) **(i)**

Statement	True	False
Day books are used in a manual accounting system to summarise transactions before they are entered in the ledgers.	✔	
Non-current assets are usually tangible items that are used in the production of goods or services, and have a life span of more than one year.	✔	
In a manual accounting system, capital introduced into the business does not require an entry in a book of prime entry.		✔

(ii)

Statement	
The capital expenditure must fit in with the business's plans and budgets.	✔
The method of funding the non-current asset must be arranged prior to purchase.	✔
The decision to buy the non-current asset is taken by the person who will use the asset.	

(iii)

the cost of the asset less its residual value	
the cost of the asset less its depreciation to date	✔
the original cost of the asset	

(b) **(i)** **Extract from non-current assets register**

Description/serial no	Acquisition date	Cost £	Depreciation charges £	Carrying amount £	Disposal proceeds £	Disposal date
Computer equipment						
PHX Laser printer	15/12/20-7	1,200.00				
Year-end 31/03/20-8			360.00	840.00		
Year-end 31/03/20-9			360.00	480.00		
Year-end 31/03/20-0			360.00	120.00		
PHX Laptop computer	26/03/20-0	750.00				
Year-end 31/03/20-0			225.00	525.00		
Vehicles						
PT17 PZV	20/05/20-7	16,000.00				
Year-end 31/03/20-8			4,000.00	12,000.00		
Year-end 31/03/20-9			3,000.00	9,000.00		
Year-end 31/03/20-0			0.00	0.00	7,500.00	14/03/20-0
PT68 ZPE	19/11/20-8	14,400.00				
Year-end 31/03/20-9			3,600.00	10,800.00		
Year-end 31/03/20-0			2,700.00	8,100.00		

(ii)

Disposals	£		£
Vehicles at cost	16,000.00	Vehicles accumulated depreciation	7,000.00
		Bank	7,500.00
		Statement of profit or loss	1,500.00
Total	16,000.00	**Total**	16,000.00

(iii)

Journal number: 72	31 March 20-0	
Account name	**Debit** £	**Credit** £
Depreciation expense	585.00	
Computer equipment accumulated depreciation		585.00

Task 2

(a) **(i)**

Valuation	
£16,220	✔
£16,420	
£23,700	
£23,860	

(ii)

Accounting principle	
Accruals	
Business entity	
Consistency	
Going concern	
Materiality	
Money measurement	
Prudence	✔

(iii)

Journal number: 32		30 June 20-5
Account name	Debit £	Credit £
Irrecoverable debts	125	
Receivables ledger control		125

(b) **(i)** One 1 July 20-4, the rent received account shows a **CREDIT** balance of £**650**.

On 30 June 20-5, the rent received account shows an adjustment for **ACCRUED INCOME** of £**700**.

(ii) £8,850

(c)

Shop expenses	£		£
Prepaid expenses reversal	120	Prepaid expenses	320
Bank	4,680	Statement of profit or loss	4,480
Total	**4,800**	**Total**	**4,800**

Task 3

(a) (i)

Error	Error disclosed by the trial balance	Error not disclosed by the trial balance
A bank payment for £284 has been debited in the payables ledger to John Peters instead of Peter Johns.		✔
The balance of sales account has been calculated incorrectly.	✔	
A bank payment for vehicle repairs has been debited to vehicles account.		✔
Drawings of £150 have been recorded in bank account but not in drawings account.	✔	

(ii)

Transaction	Assets	Liabilities	Capital
Matt takes out a bank loan to buy a new computer for use in the business.	Increase	Increase	No effect
Matt makes a bank payment to a credit supplier, which increases his overdraft.	No effect	No effect	No effect

(b)

Errors	Payables ledger control account		Payables' accounts		No effect
	Debit £	Credit £	Debit £	Credit £	✔
The account of Manners & Co, £175, has been written off in receivables ledger, but has not been recorded in receivables ledger control account.		175			
The total column of sales returns day book has been overcast by £200.	200				
Discounts allowed to trade receivables of £58 have been entered on the wrong side of receivables ledger control account.		116			
A bank payment for £250 from Quin Ltd has been entered in the receivables ledger account of Quinn & Co.					✔

(c)

Trial balance for Alexandra Lukac as at 31 December 20-3				
Account name	Ledger balances		Adjustments	
	Dr £	Cr £	Dr £	Cr £
Administration expenses	53,941			
Bank	5,200			2,400
Capital		56,500		2,000
Depreciation charges	15,150			
Drawings	12,185			
Irrecoverable debts	395			
Machinery at cost	158,500			
Machinery accumulated depreciation		42,300		
Office expenses	31,046			
Opening inventory	5,212			
Payables ledger control		11,147	1,000	
Purchases	146,038			
Receivables ledger control	20,868			
Rent	10,380		2,400	
Sales		365,242		
Selling expenses	22,346			
VAT		5,072		
Closing inventory: Statement of financial position			6,490	
Closing inventory: Statement of profit or loss				6,490
Suspense		1,000	2,000	1,000
TOTAL	481,261	481,261	11,890	11,890

(d)

Extract of the trial balance of Linda Goode as at 31 December 20-3		
	Dr £	**Cr** £
Prepaid income		500
Accrued expenses		425
Depreciation expense	2,250	
Disposal of non-current assets	850	
Irrecoverable debts	345	
Discounts received		164

Task 4

(a)   (i)

Statement	True	False
Partnership profits are always split equally between the partners.		✔
In a partnership, a partner's capital account is normally fixed and only alters if permanent capital changes.	✔	
In a partnership, a partner's current account is credited with interest on drawings.		✔
The accounting rules for a partnership are often set out in a partnership agreement.	✔	

(ii)

Statement	
Profit for the year + interest on drawings – partner's salary + interest on capital	
Profit for the year – interest on drawings – partner's salary – interest on capital	
Profit for the year + interest on drawings – partner's salary – interest on capital	✔
Profit for the year + interest on drawings + partner's salary – interest on capital	

(iii)

The purpose of a statement of profit or loss is to show …	
the profitability of the business.	✔
the cash position of the business.	
that there are no errors in the accounting system.	
the assets and liabilities of the business at a given date.	

(b)   **(i)**

Journal number: 32		31 March 20-1
	Debit £	**Credit** £
Drawings	360	
Purchases*		300
VAT		60

* **Note:** alternatively, credit sales account.

(ii)   £27,893

(iii)

Capital			
Account name	**£**	**Account name**	**£**
Drawings	*23,910	Balance b/d	60,500
Balance c/d	64,483	Profit for the year	27,893
Total	88,393	Total	88,393

* **Note:** £23,550 + £360 goods for own use.

(iv)

Phoebe's Motor Parts Statement of financial position as at 31 March 20-1			
	Cost £	Accumulated depreciation £	Carrying amount £
Non-current assets	30,200	6,870	23,330
Current assets			
Inventory		12,035	
Trade receivables		10,047	
Bank		31,164	
Total current assets		53,246	
Current liabilities			
Trade payables	10,157		
VAT	*1,936		
Total current liabilities		12,093	
Net current liabilities			41,153
Net assets			64,483

* £1,876 + £60 from drawings

Task 5

This task is about accounting principles, qualities of useful financial information, and interpreting financial statements using profitability ratios.

(a) **(i)** Identify the accounting principle being described by each of the following statements.

Statement	Accounting principle
When preparing financial statements for a business, the presumption is that it will continue to trade in the foreseeable future.	Going concern
The private house of the owner of the business is not recorded on the statement of financial position of the business.	Business entity
The value of goods purchased for resale but not yet paid for at the year-end is included in purchases for the year.	Accruals
Low value non-current assets are expensed to the statement of profit or loss.	Materiality

(ii)

Groups	
Investors, employees, managers of the business	
Lenders, other creditors, customers	
Lenders, existing and potential investors, other creditors	✔
Customers, lenders, potential investors	

(b)

Statement	True	False
A gross profit margin of 20% is the equivalent of a gross profit mark-up of 25%.	✔	
Professional scepticism when interpreting financial information includes having a questioning mind and making a critical assessment.	✔	
An increase in the amount of mark-up applied to goods purchased for resale will result in a lower gross profit.		✔
Comparisons of ratios can be made with a different business, a different time period, and an industry standard.	✔	

(c)   (i)

Net profit margin (%)	4.97%
Return on capital employed (%)	13.72%

(ii)

Statement	True	False
The increase could have been caused by sales revenue rising during the year.		✔
The increase could have been caused by higher expenditure on selling expenses during the year.	✔	
The increase in the current year's percentage shows improvement when compared with the previous year.		✔

(d)   **Scenario 1**

	Increase	Unchanged	Decrease
Return on capital employed			✔
Cost of sales/revenue percentage	✔		

Scenario 2

	Increase	Unchanged	Decrease
Gross profit margin		✔	
Net profit margin			✔

Task 6

(a)

£13,500	
£16,200	✔
£116,800	

(b)

If the closing inventory figure reported by the accounting software is higher than the physical inventory check, this could lead to gross profit being **overstated** and current assets being **overstated**.

(c) **(i)**   £112,900

(ii)   £73,385

(iii) £39,515

(iv)   £8,425

(v)

Administration expenses			
Account name	**£**	**Account name**	**£**
Prepaid expenses reversal	140	Statement of profit or loss	23,960
Administration expenses day book	23,610		
Accrued expenses	210		
Total	23,960	Total	23,960

(vi)   £15,555

for your notes

for your notes

for your notes

for your notes

for your notes

for your notes

for your notes

for your notes

for your notes

for your notes

for your notes

for your notes

for your notes

for your notes

for your notes

for your notes

for your notes

for your notes

for your notes

for your notes